EDEXCEL GCSE SCIENCE

Early Starters Book

Series Editor: Mark Levesley

Richard Grime

Miles Hudson

Nigel Saunders

A PEARSON COMPANY

Edexcel GCSE Science: Early Starters Book
Picture Credits

The publisher would like to thank the following for their kind permission to reproduce their photographs:

(Key: b-bottom; c-centre; l-left; r-right; t-top)

Alamy Images: David J. Green - financial 52c, Evan Bowen-Jones 29, Leslie Garland Picture Library 42b, Susan E. Degginger 30b; **Corbis:** Gavin Wickham; Eye Ubiquitous 51l, Louise Gubb 26t; **DK Images:** Dorling Kindersley 10c, Harry Taylor 31br; **ESA:** C. Carreau 39; **Mary Evans Picture Library:** Illustrated London News 42t; **FLIR:** 52bl, 52br; **Gemini Observatory/Association of Universities for Research in Astronomy:** 43; **GeoScience Features Picture Library:** 26b; **Getty Images:** AFP 16t, JIJI PRESS / AFP 12t, Roy Stevens / Time Life Pictures 50t; **Image Quest Marine:** 16br; **iStockphoto:** Antti-Pekka Lehtinen 9, Christopher Jones 7c; **Jonny Keeling:** 14t; **Kobal Collection Ltd:** 20TH CENTURY FOX / THE KOBAL COLLECTION 48, UNIVERSAL TV 54t; **Mark Levesley:** 17cl, 17cr; **NASA:** Akira Fujii and Infrared Astronomical Satellite 49, ESA / NASA / JPL / University of Arizona 24t, JPL-Caltech 46br, NASA / JPL / Space Science Institute 24bl, NASA / The Hubble Heritage Team / STScI / AURA 24br; **Natural History Museum Picture Library:** 10t; **Nature Picture Library:** HERMANN BREHM 13cl; **NHPA Ltd / Photoshot Holdings:** Dave Watts 27t; **Norfolk Skyview:** Mike Page 44; **Oscar & Dehn Ltd:** 51r; **Pearson Education Ltd:** Digital Vision 7t, 16bl, Fancy. Veer. Corbis 7b, Photodisc. C Squared Studios 6b, Photodisc. Siede Preis Photography 31t, Trevor Clifford 30c, 34c, 36l; **Reproduced by permission of The Royal Society of Chemistry:** Visual Elements –Chemical Data – Radium (http:/ / www.rsc.org / chemsoc / visualelements / PAGES / data / radium_data.html); 54b; **Reuters:** Osman Orsal 6t; **Rex Features:** Patrick Frilet 28; **Robert Harding World Imagery:** Cosmo Condina 38t; **Science Photo Library Ltd:** 47l, BJORN RORSLETT 47r, CCI ARCHIVES 46bl, EYE OF SCIENCE 22c, J.C. REVY, ISM 8b, JAMES KING-HOLMES 20t, JIM AMOS 33, JOHN READER 30t, L. WILLATT, EAST ANGLIAN REGIONAL GENETICS SERVICE 18b, MAX ALEXANDER / LORD EGREMONT 40, MERLIN TUTTLE / BAT CONSERVATION INTERNATIONAL 18t, POWER AND SYRED 18c, SHEILA TERRY 46t, SIMON FRASER / RVI, NEWCASTLE-UPON-TYNE 22b; **Thinkstock:** iStockphoto 8t, 13cr, 14cl, 14cr, 14b, 31l, 32, 34t, 36t, 50b, 52tr; **University of North Carolina:** Professor Joseph DeSimone 22t.

All other images © Pearson Education

Every effort has been made to trace the copyright holders and we apologise in advance for any unintentional omissions.
We would be pleased to insert the appropriate acknowledgement in any subsequent edition of this publication.

Contents

How to use this Early Starters Book   4

What to expect from your full science student book   6

Biology 1: Influences on life

Topic B1.1: Variation

B1.1: Classification	8
B1.2: Vertebrates and invertebrates	10
B1.3: Species	12
B1.4: Variation	14
B1.5: Variation: practice CA (not included)	
B1.6: Evolution	16
B1.7: Genes	18
B1.8: Explaining inheritance	20
B1.9: Genetic disorders	22

Chemistry 1: Chemistry in our world

Topic C1.1: The Earth's sea and atmosphere

C1.1: The early atmosphere	24
C1.2: A changing atmosphere	26
C1.3: Oxygen in the atmosphere: practice CA (not included)	
C1.4: The atmosphere today	28

Topic C1.2: Materials from the Earth

C1.5: Rocks and their formation	30
C1.6: Limestone and its uses	32
C1.7: Thermal decomposition of carbonates: practice CA (not included)	
C1.8: Chemical reaction	34
C1.9: Reactions of calcium compounds	36

Physics 1: Universal physics

Topic P1.1: Visible light and the Solar System

P1.1: The Solar System	38
P1.2: Refracting telescopes	40
P1.3: Lenses: practice CA (not included)	
P1.4: Reflecting telescopes	42
P1.5: Waves	44

Topic P1.2: The electromagnetic spectrum

P1.6: Beyond the visible	46
P1.7: The electromagnetic spectrum	48
P1.8: Electromagnetic dangers	50
P1.9: Using electromagnetic radiation	52
P1.10: Ionising radiation	54

More resources for your course   56

How to use this Early Starters Book

B1.1 Classification

 How are organisms classified?

Natural sea sponges can be used for cleaning but many people assume that they are plants. Sponges are actually animals and the 'sponge' that we use is a very soft skeleton.

Until about 1700 most scientists thought that sponges were plants. This was due to the Greek thinker Aristotle (384 BCE to 322 BCE), who was one of the first people to sort organisms into groups based on their **characteristics** (what they look like). This process is called **classification**. For Aristotle, organisms that did not move were plants.

1 Why did Aristotle think that sponges were plants?
2 What is classification?

A Sea sponges grow on the seabed, attached to rocks.

Today, scientists look at the cells of organisms to decide whether they are in the **plant kingdom** or the **animal kingdom**. Most plants have cells that contain **chloroplasts**. These are structures in the cell that absorb light to power **photosynthesis** (the process by which plants make their own food). Plant cells also have cellulose **cell walls** to help support the cells.

ResultsPlus Watch Out!
Some students confuse cell walls with cell membranes. All cells have cell membranes but they don't all have cell walls.

B Plant cells

3 a What process do plants use to make their own food?
b What part of a plant cell allows this process to happen?

Animal cells do not contain chloroplasts and do not have cell walls. Unlike plants, most animals have nerves running through their bodies. The nerves carry information and form the **nervous system**.

Progress questions can be used to check understanding as you work through the course.

These boxes provide plenty of examiner tips on common mistakes students make in their exams.

Topic B1.1: Variation

Other kingdoms

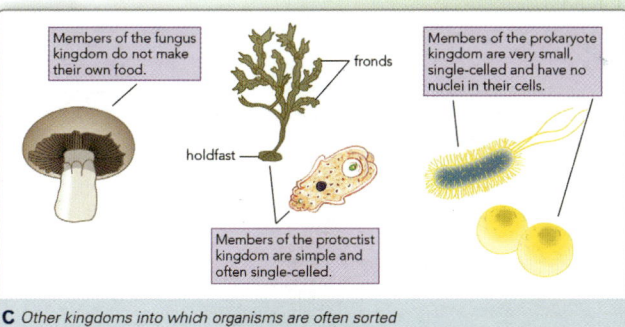

C *Other kingdoms into which organisms are often sorted*

Fungi (members of the **fungus kingdom**) used to be classified as plants because they had similar growth habits to plants. However, they lack chloroplasts and their cell walls are not made of cellulose.

Euglena are single-celled organisms that have features of both plant and animal cells. they are a type of **algae** and like all algae (which include seaweeds) they are in the **protoctist kingdom**. The protoctist kingdom contains all the organisms that can't fit into one of the other four kingdoms.

Bacteria are single-celled organisms, like many protoctists. However, all bacteria lack nuclei and so are in the **prokaryote kingdom**.

There is no kingdom for **viruses** because most scientists do not think of them as being alive. When a virus particle gets into a living cell, it changes the way in which that cell works and causes it to make copies of the virus. However, the actual virus particle is not living.

Not all scientists agree on the five kingdoms. Some classify organisms into six kingdoms (prokaryotes are split into two kingdoms). There is also an idea to combine protoctists, fungi, plants and animals into one super-kingdom, called a 'domain'.

6 A dictionary publisher needs definitions of the words 'plant' and 'animal'. Write definitions for the dictionary.

Skills spotlight

In a successful argument, evidence is presented for and against an idea, and then used to reach a decision. Construct an argument for classifying *Euglena* as a plant or an animal or neither.

4 Seaweeds do not have cellulose cell walls but do photosynthesise.
a Suggest why seaweeds were once thought to be plants.
H b Give one reason why they are no longer classified as plants.

H 5 Viruses do not have a nucleus and nor do bacteria. So why are viruses not in the prokaryote kingdom with bacteria?

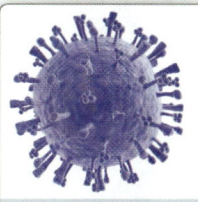

D *A virus particle*

Learning Outcomes

1.1 Describe the characteristics that are used to classify organisms in the plant or animal kingdoms: a most plants have chloroplasts and the ability to make their own food b most animals are complex organisms that have nervous systems

H 1.2 Demonstrate an understanding of the issues surrounding the classification of fungi, bacteria, algae and viruses:
a fungi are not classified as plants because they lack chloroplasts and a cellulose cell wall and are placed in their own kingdom b bacteria lack nuclei and are placed in the prokaryote kingdom c algae have features of both plants and animals (as illustrated by *Euglena*) and are placed in the protoctist kingdom d viruses are regarded by most scientists as non-living and therefore are not placed in any kingdom

HSW 11 Present information, develop an argument and draw a conclusion, using scientific, technical and mathematical language, and ICT tools

Can you name a poisonous mammal?

'Skills spotlight' boxes build How Science Works skills.

Higher-tier only material, questions and outcomes are clearly identified with a small H icon.

The last progress question on every spread is designed to provide you with an opportunity to develop your written communication skills.

Learning outcomes are taken straight from the specification to make it clear what is needed for the exam.

What else to expect from your full Science student book

As well as lots more pages like the ones in this *Early Starters Book*, making it clear exactly what you need to learn for your exams, the full version of the book will also contain:

- **Practice Controlled Assessments** so that you can build the skills you need to fulfil your potential in the controlled assessment part of your course

- **ResultsPlus exam practice materials**, including pages and pages of sample exam questions written by the examiners, and sample student answers at different levels

- **Your course and controlled assessment explained**: chapters written by the Edexcel science team to explain exactly how your course, the exams and your controlled assessment will work, so you're fully prepared!

Spreads on the specification practicals can be used as practice controlled assessments.

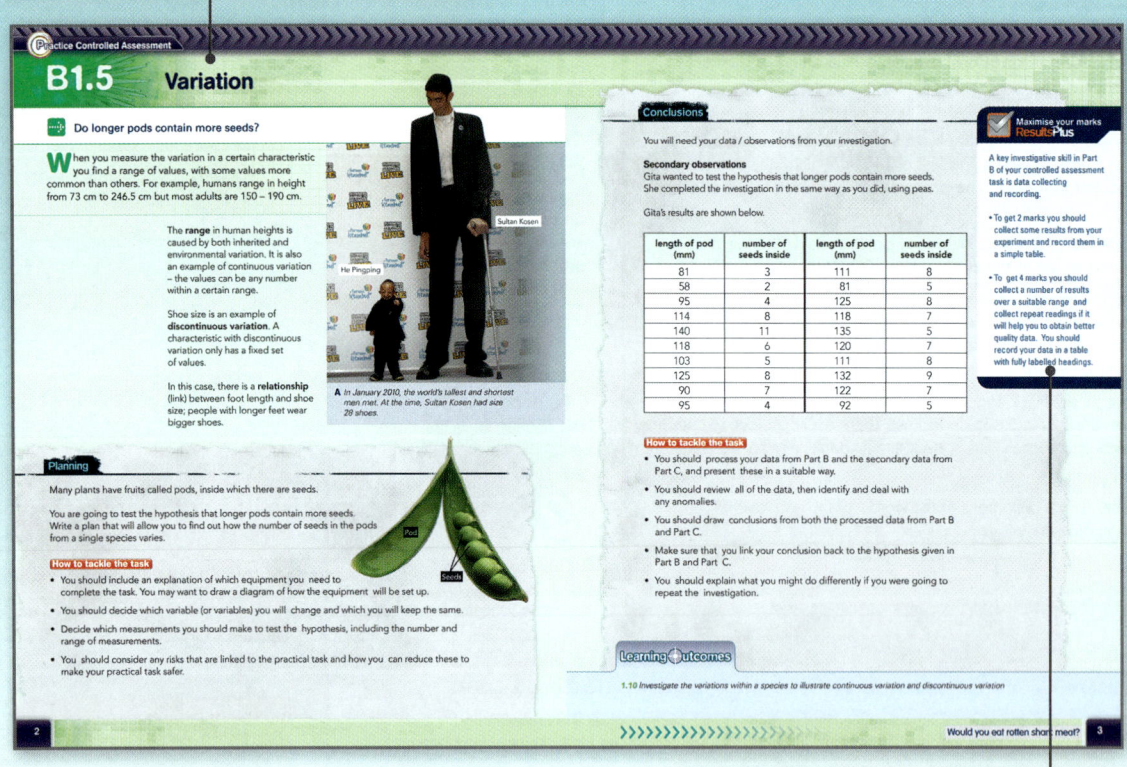

The spreads provide detailed guidance on how to improve your marks in the different parts of the controlled assessment.

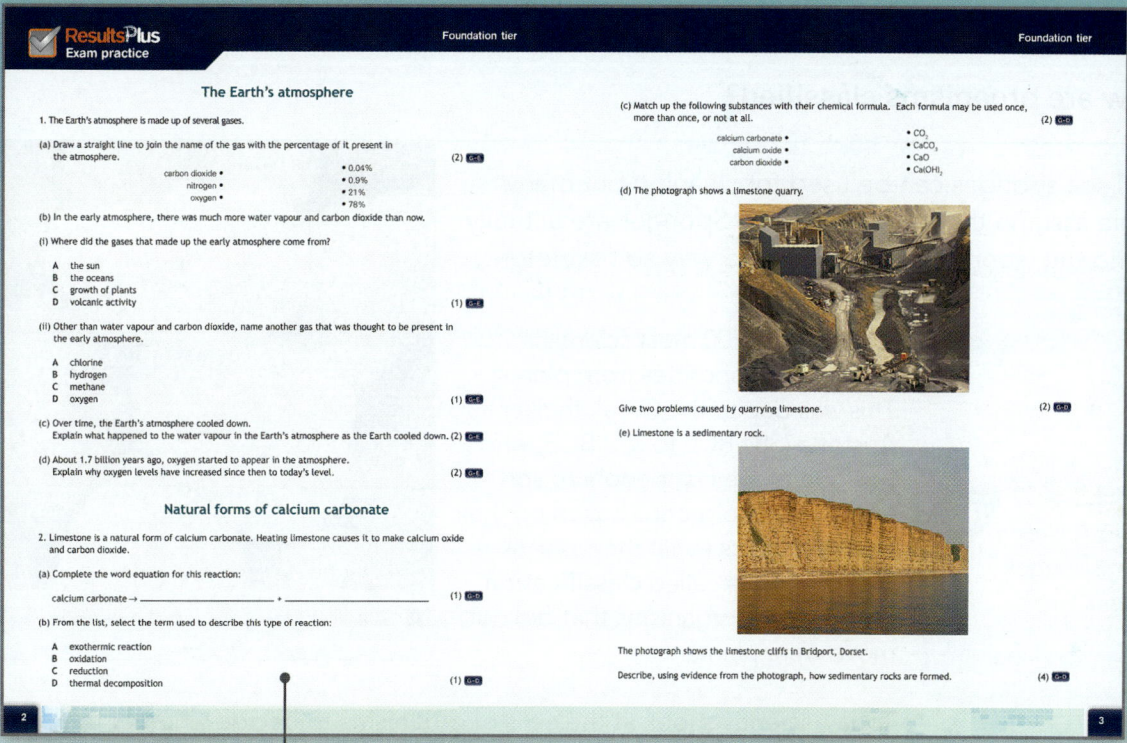

Exam practice spreads provide a large bank of the new question types you will encounter in your exams, all written by the examiner team.

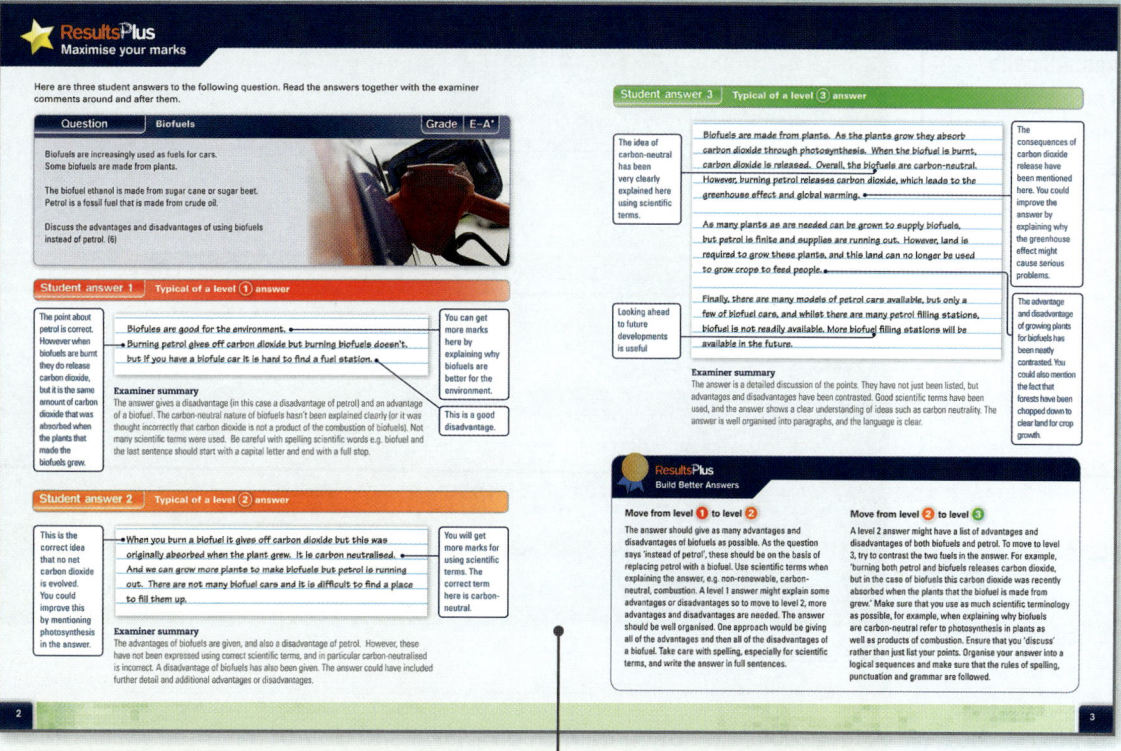

Maximise your marks pages focus on exemplar student answers to the extended writing questions and make it clear how to progress up through the mark scheme to improve your marks.

B1.1 Classification

 How are organisms classified?

Natural sea sponges can be used for cleaning but many people assume that they are plants. Sponges are actually animals and the 'sponge' that we use is a very soft skeleton.

A *Sea sponges grow on the seabed, attached to rocks.*

Until about 1700 most scientists thought that sponges were plants. This was due to the Greek thinker Aristotle (384 BCE to 322 BCE) who was one of the first people to sort organisms into groups based on their **characteristics** (what they look like). This process is called **classification**. For Aristotle, organisms that did not move were plants.

1 Why did Aristotle think that sponges were plants?

2 What is classification?

ResultsPlus Watch Out!

Some students confuse cell walls with cell membranes. All cells have cell membranes but they don't all have cell walls.

Today, scientists look at the cells of organisms to decide whether they are in the **plant kingdom** or the **animal kingdom**. Most plants have cells that contain **chloroplasts**. These are structures in the cell that absorb light to power **photosynthesis** (the process by which plants make their own food). Plant cells also have cellulose **cell walls** to help support the cells.

B *Plant cells*

3 a What process do plants use to make their own food?
b What part of a plant cell allows this process to happen?

Animal cells do not contain chloroplasts and do not have cell walls. Unlike plants, most animals have nerves running through their bodies. The nerves carry information and form the **nervous system**.

Other kingdoms

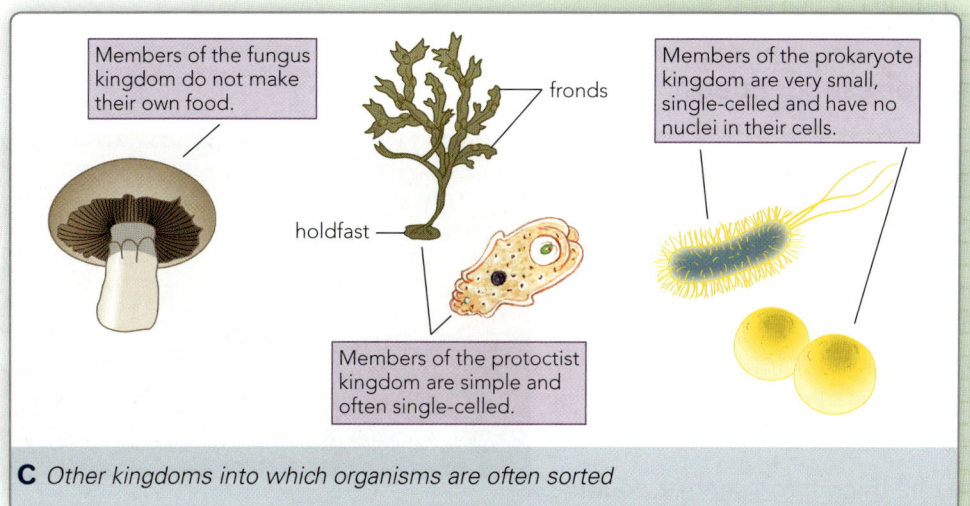

C Other kingdoms into which organisms are often sorted

Fungi (members of the **fungus kingdom**) used to be classified as plants because they had similar growth habits to plants. However, they lack chloroplasts and their cell walls are not made of cellulose.

Euglena are single-celled organisms that have features of both plant and animal cells. They are a type of **algae** and like all algae (which include seaweeds) they are in the **protoctist kingdom**. The protoctist kingdom contains all the organisms that can't fit into one of the other four kingdoms.

Bacteria are single-celled organisms, like many protoctists. However, all bacteria lack nuclei and so are in the **prokaryote kingdom**.

There is no kingdom for **viruses** because most scientists do not think of them as being alive. When a virus particle gets into a living cell, it changes the way that cell works and causes it to make copies of the virus. However, the actual virus particle is not living.

Not all scientists agree on the five kingdoms. Some classify organisms into six kingdoms (prokaryotes are split into two kingdoms). There is also an idea to combine protoctists, fungi, plants and animals into one super-kingdom, called a 'domain'.

6 A dictionary publisher needs definitions of the words 'plant' and 'animal'. Write definitions for the dictionary.

Skills spotlight

In a successful argument, evidence is presented for and against an idea, and then used to reach a decision. Construct an argument for classifying *Euglena* as a plant or an animal or neither.

4 Seaweeds do not have cellulose cell walls but do photosynthesise.
a Suggest why seaweeds were once thought to be plants.
H b Give one reason why they are no longer classified as plants.

H 5 Viruses do not have a nucleus and nor do bacteria. So why are viruses not in the prokaryote kingdom with bacteria?

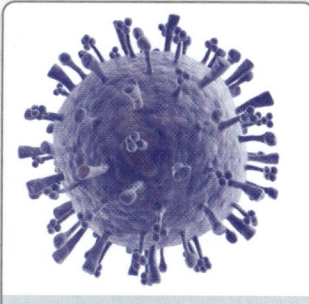

D A virus particle

Learning Outcomes

1.1 Describe the characteristics that are used to classify organisms in the plant or animal kingdoms: **a** most plants have chloroplasts and the ability to make their own food **b** most animals are complex organisms that have nervous systems

H 1.2 Demonstrate an understanding of the issues surrounding the classification of fungi, bacteria, algae and viruses:
a fungi are not classified as plants because they lack chloroplasts and a cellulose cell wall and are placed in their own kingdom
b bacteria lack nuclei and are placed in the prokaryote kingdom **c** algae have features of both plants and animals (as illustrated by *Euglena*) and are placed in the protoctist kingdom **d** viruses are regarded by most scientists as non-living and therefore are not placed in any kingdom

HSW 11 Present information, develop an argument and draw a conclusion, using scientific, technical and mathematical language, and ICT tools

Can you name a poisonous mammal?

B1.2 Vertebrates and invertebrates

 How is the animal kingdom subdivided?

English settlers in Australia discovered duck-billed platypuses in 1797. Dead specimens were sent back to England but scientists thought they were a practical joke! When the platypus was confirmed as being real, scientists could not agree how to classify a poisonous, furry animal with a duck's beak, a beaver's tail, an otter's feet and a lizard's skeleton shape, that lays leathery eggs.

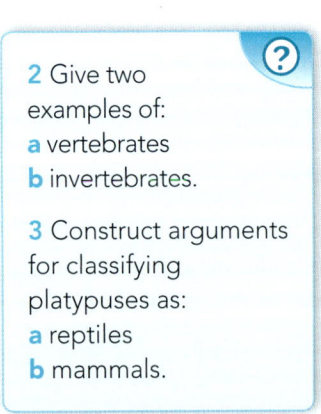

A This duck-billed platypus was sent to the Natural History Museum at the end of the eighteenth century. The scientist who examined it tried to remove the bill with a pair of scissors because he thought it was a hoax.

- scissor marks
- Males have a 'spur' on their hind legs, which contains a poison.
- Females have mammary glands that produce milk but these glands do not have nipples.

The one thing that scientists could agree on was that platypuses were **vertebrates**. Vertebrates are animals that have a backbone (a series of small bones called **vertebrae**).

1 a What is a backbone?
b What is its purpose?

The backbone supports the animal. It also protects a bundle of nerves, called the spinal cord, which is an important part of the nervous system.

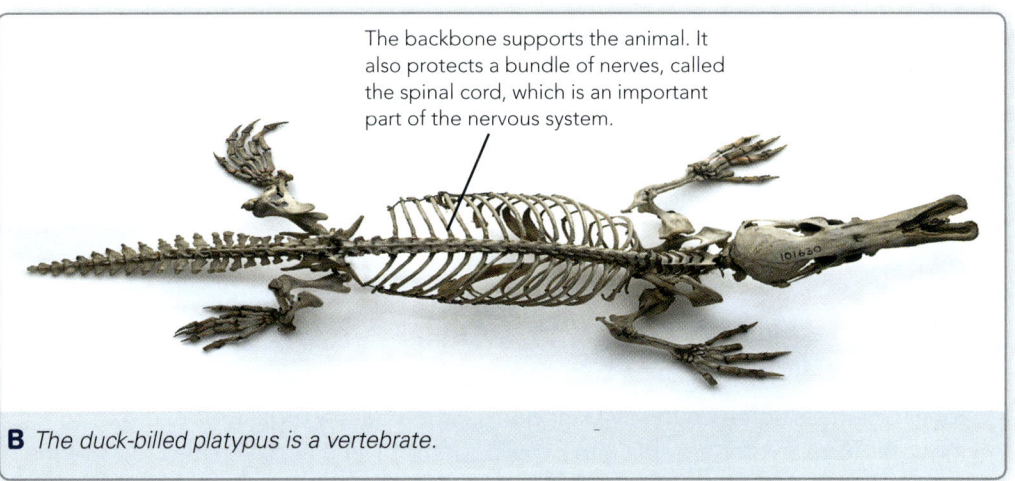

B The duck-billed platypus is a vertebrate.

Animals that do not have a backbone are called **invertebrates**. The vertebrate and invertebrate groups are both divided into smaller groups.

2 Give two examples of:
a vertebrates
b invertebrates.

3 Construct arguments for classifying platypuses as:
a reptiles
b mammals.

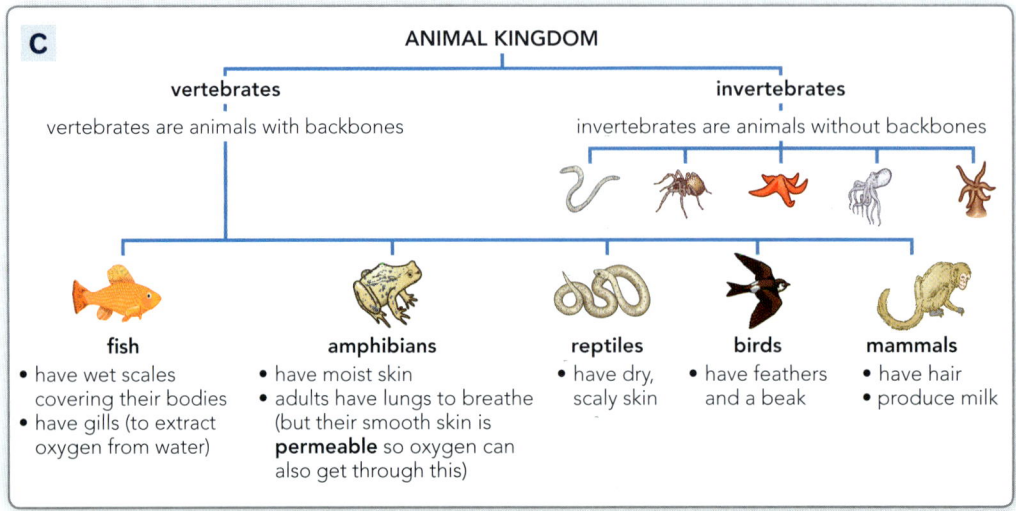

C
ANIMAL KINGDOM
- **vertebrates**: vertebrates are animals with backbones
- **invertebrates**: invertebrates are animals without backbones

- **fish**: have wet scales covering their bodies; have gills (to extract oxygen from water)
- **amphibians**: have moist skin; adults have lungs to breathe (but their smooth skin is **permeable** so oxygen can also get through this)
- **reptiles**: have dry, scaly skin
- **birds**: have feathers and a beak
- **mammals**: have hair; produce milk

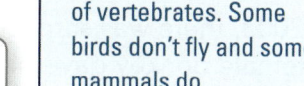

Topic B1.1: Variation

The different groups of vertebrates in Figure C are divided into smaller and smaller groups with fewer members. As the groups get smaller, the members of the groups become more closely related and have more characteristics in common.

The last group contains a single type of organism called a **species**. Species have Latin names containing two words; the names of the last two groups that the organism is in.

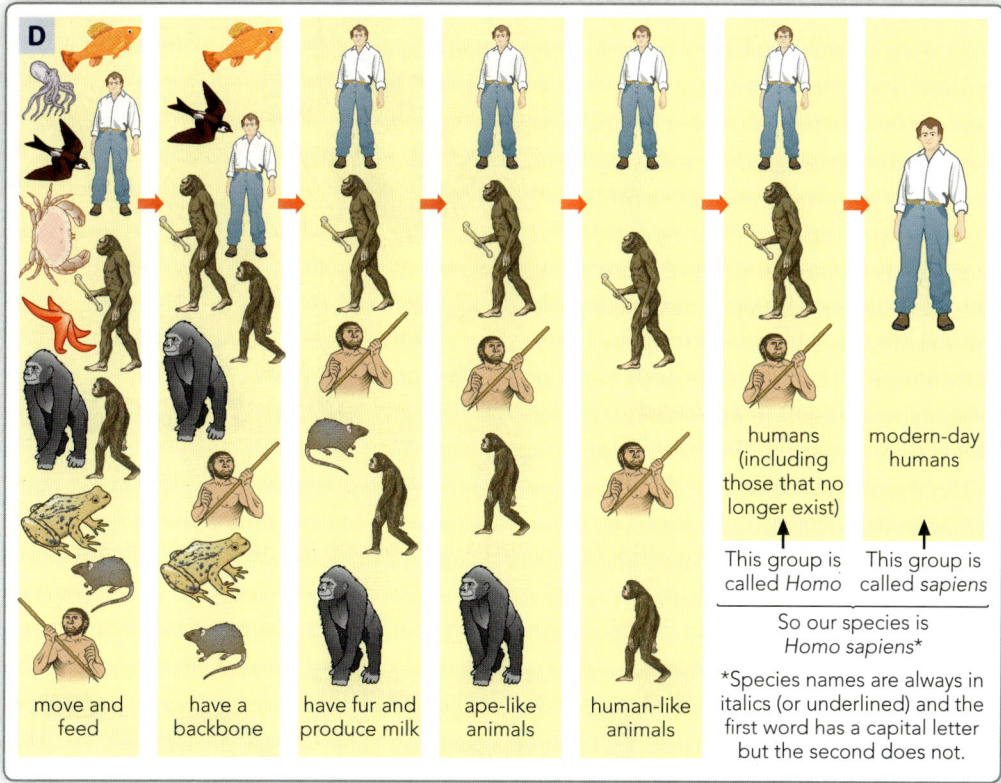

D

| move and feed | have a backbone | have fur and produce milk | ape-like animals | human-like animals | humans (including those that no longer exist) | modern-day humans |

This group is called *Homo*   This group is called *sapiens*

So our species is *Homo sapiens**

*Species names are always in italics (or underlined) and the first word has a capital letter but the second does not.

ResultsPlus
Watch Out!

Don't use 'flight' as a difference between birds and other groups of vertebrates. Some birds don't fly and some mammals do.

Skills spotlight

A Venn diagram is a way of showing the relationships between different groups of things. Figure C shows that all invertebrates are animals. Draw a Venn diagram showing all the groups mentioned on these two pages.

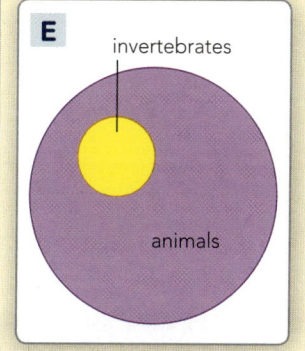

E
invertebrates
animals

4 List some groups that mice are found in.

5 What is the species name for humans?

6 From where does an organism get the first of its two Latin names?

7 Over the centuries many different classification systems have been tried. Evaluate a classification system for vertebrates based only on the number of legs.

Learning Outcomes

1.3 Describe the main characteristics of vertebrates and invertebrates

1.4 Explain how vertebrate animals are classified into five groups:
 a most fish have wet scales and gills
 b most amphibians have smooth, moist, permeable skin
 c most reptiles have dry, scaly skin
 d most birds have feathers and a beak
 e most mammals have hair and produce milk

HSW 11 Present information using scientific conventions and symbols

What is a zedonk?

B1.3 Species

 Why can classifying species be difficult?

In 2003, there was surprise at a Japanese safari park when a female donkey gave birth to a foal with stripes! Its father had been one of the park's zebras.

A The 'zedonk' hybrid foal with its mother.

1 American robins and British robins cannot interbreed. Suggest why not.

2 What is a hybrid?

3 Why can't a zedonk be classified as a species?

Looking from left to right in Figure B, you will see that the organisms in each box get more and more closely related – they have more in common with each other. The two boxes in the last column show individual **species**. A species is a group of organisms that can **interbreed** (reproduce with one another) to produce offspring that are **fertile** (able to reproduce).

Two closely related species can often breed and produce **hybrids**. Hybrids are neither one species nor another and so cannot be classified.

B Donkey and zebra classification

Skills spotlight

Scientists tell each other about their work by writing papers, which are published in journals (a type of magazine). Papers are usually peer-reviewed, which means that other scientists read the papers and say whether their scientific evidence is good enough to be published. State one advantage and one disadvantage of peer-reviewing.

Hybrids are usually infertile but not always. Mallard ducks can breed with other closely-related species to produce fertile offspring. These offspring then breed with other hybrids or mallard ducks or closely-related ducks. This produces ducks with a continuous range of characteristics, rather than separate species.

Neighbouring populations of the same species may have slightly different characteristics but still interbreed. Sometimes there is a chain of different populations that can all breed with their neighbouring populations but the two populations at either end of the chain cannot interbreed. The chain often forms a ring shape and so these organisms are called **ring species**.

Topic B1.1: Variation

Difficulties with classification

Hybrids cannot be classified as a species and it is hard to divide ring species into separate species. The gulls in Figure C are traditionally considered to be two species - *Larus fuscus* (the lesser black-backed gull) and *Larus argentatus* (the European herring gull). However, classifying the gulls between these two is difficult because there is a gradual change of characteristics between the two species.

Naming a species

An organism's scientific name has two Latin words. This is called the binomial system. Organisms that share the first word in their name (e.g. Equus, Larus) are closely related. Scientists can tell from the name whether two organisms are closely related.

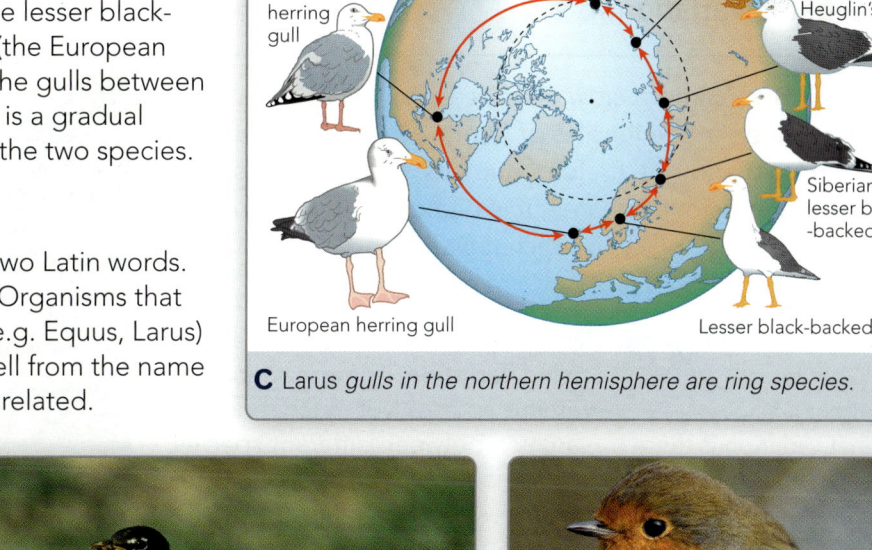

C *Larus gulls in the northern hemisphere are ring species.*

The **binomial system** is also useful because organisms with the same common names may actually be different species. For example, a robin in America is not the same bird as a robin in the UK. The system is agreed by scientists all over the world to allow them to communicate clearly, whatever their language.

D *An American robin*, Turdus migratorius

E *A UK robin*, Erithacus rubecula

4 Suggest two gulls in Figure C that cannot interbreed.

5 Why might it be difficult to identify the species of a duck on a local pond?

6 Why is it hard to divide populations that form ring species into separate species?

7 Why is the binomial system so useful?

8 The binomial system is like our system of first names and family names. Compare and contrast the two systems.

ResultsPlus
Watch Out!

You are not expected to remember the Latin names for organisms. If you need them in an exam, you will be given them. Just make sure you copy them carefully!

Learning Outcomes

1.5 Define the term species as organisms that are capable of interbreeding to produce fertile offspring

1.6 Demonstrate an understanding of why scientists around the world use the binomial system as a basis for naming species

1.8 Demonstrate an understanding of how accurate classification may be complicated by: **a** hybridisation **b** ring species **c** variation within a species

HSW 14 Describe how scientists share data and discuss new ideas, and how over time this process helps to reduce uncertainties and revise scientific theories

How big is a giant rat?

13

B1.4 Variation

What is variation?

In 2009, a BBC camera crew discovered a new species of giant rat, deep in the jungles of Papua New Guinea. It was 82 cm long and not afraid of humans. While scientists are agreeing its scientific name, it is being called the Bosavi woolly rat (after the place in which it was found).

> **1 a** What is variation?
> **b** What variation is there between the rats in Figure B?

Differences in characteristics are called **variation**. There is variation within a species but much more variation between different species. This variation within a species can make classification difficult.

A A Bosavi woolly rat

B Rats of the same species show great variation. Great variation within a species can be confusing and make classification difficult.

Scientists must make sure that any 'new' organism is not just a hybrid or due to variation in a known species. They do this by finding more than one of the organisms.

From the Bosavi woolly rats that have been found, scientists can tell that they are closely related to other 'hairy rats' because they share many characteristics. However, Bosavi woolly rats have sufficient variations in those characteristics to show that they are a new species.

Keys

To identify different species, you can use a **key**. Figure C shows a key for rats.

> **2 a** What evidence is there that the woolly rat is a different species to the rats in Figure B?
> **b** How might further evidence be collected to show that they are different species?
>
> **3** Why do scientists need to find more than one example of a 'new' organism?
>
> **4** Use the key to identify which rat species is shown in Figure B.

Statement:	Next step:
1 The animal has a thick, bushy tail.	squirrel
The animal has a tail that is covered with layers of skin, which look like scales.	go to 2
2 It has a band of hair that is longer than the rest of the fur.	crested rat
Its fur is all the same length.	go to 3
3 It has a short tail.	groove-toothed rat
It has a long tail.	go to 4
4 Its tail is shorter than its body.	brown rat (*Rattus norvegicus*)
Its tail is longer than its body.	black rat (*Rattus rattus*)

C To use the key, pick the correct statement from the first box and follow the 'next step' instructions. Carry on doing this until you reach a name.

Topic B1.1: Variation

The importance of classification

Accurate classification allows biologists to:
- easily identify existing species and new species
- see how organisms are related
- identify areas of greater and lesser **biodiversity**.

Biodiversity is a measure of the total number of different species in an area. To count the species you need to be able to identify them, which can be tricky if species are very similar to one another. The more accurate your classification system, the easier identification becomes.

Biodiversity is important because we obtain many products from living things (e.g. foods, medicines). The more species there are, the more choices we will have, both now and in the future. Biodiverse areas are also much better at recovering from natural disasters (e.g. floods) than less diverse areas.

Many biologists think that areas of greater biodiversity ('biodiversity hotspots') are the ones that need the most time and money spent on trying to conserve them because this will result in a greater number of species being conserved.

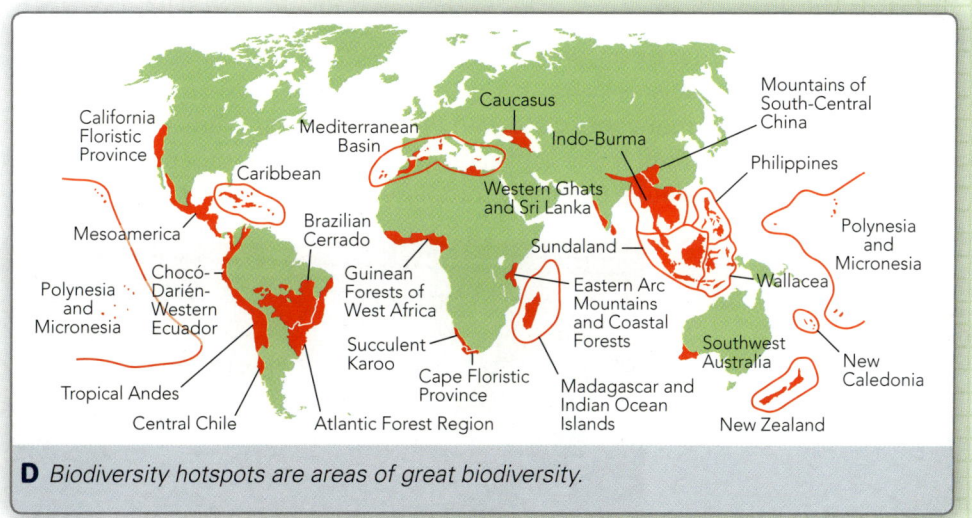

D Biodiversity hotspots are areas of great biodiversity.

ResultsPlus Watch Out!

Students often make mistakes by thinking keys are easy and answering the questions quickly. Go through the sentences twice to check your answer so you don't make silly mistakes.

Skills spotlight

The paragraph at the top of page 24 contains secondary data because the person using it is not the person who collected the data. The information comes from a TV programme. The people who wrote the TV programme used primary data because they found the rats. Suggest one advantage and one disadvantage of using secondary data.

H 5 How does classification make it easier to measure biodiversity?

H 6 Why is it important to protect biodiversity hotspots?

7 Design a key to identify some farm animals. Try to include animals from different species and from the same species.

Learning Outcomes

1.9 Construct and use keys to show how species can be identified

1.8 Demonstrate an understanding of how accurate classification may be complicated by: **a** hybridisation **b** ring species **c** variation within a species

H 1.7 Demonstrate an understanding of why accurate classification is needed to identify, study and conserve species, and recognise areas of greater biodiversity

HSW 1 Explain how scientific data is collected and analysed

How tall can people grow?

15

B1.6 Evolution

  What is Darwin's theory of evolution?

Shark tissues contain TMAO, a chemical that is poisonous to humans in high concentrations. Greenland sharks, found in the Arctic Ocean, contain much higher amounts of TMAO than other sharks because it is a natural antifreeze. This makes them poisonous to humans.

A Hákarl, made from rotten shark, is a food speciality in Iceland. Burying the flesh in the ground for a few months gets rid of the TMAO poison.

All organisms are **adapted** to their surroundings – they have variations in their characteristics that allow them to survive in their **habitats**.

Organisms from polar regions, like Greenland sharks and polar bears, are adapted to the cold. Organisms living near deep-sea **hydrothermal vents** cope with the opposite problem. Hot fluids, at more than 350°C, come out of these vents and cool quickly. The organisms living here must cope with big temperature changes, complete darkness and huge pressures.

- small ears to stop it losing too much heat
- white fur for camouflage
- thick fur for insulation
- thick layer of blubber (fat) under the skin for insulation
- large feet to spread out its weight and stop it sinking into the snow - also good for swimming
- rough soles to grip the ice

C Polar bear adaptations

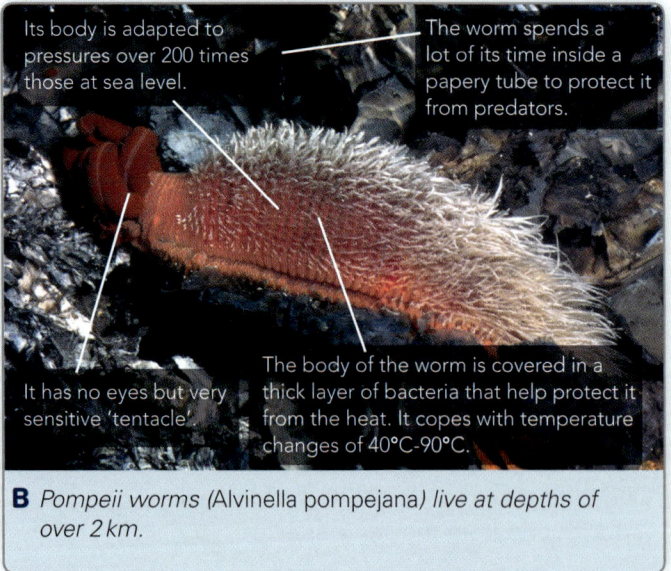

- Its body is adapted to pressures over 200 times those at sea level.
- The worm spends a lot of its time inside a papery tube to protect it from predators.
- It has no eyes but very sensitive 'tentacle'.
- The body of the worm is covered in a thick layer of bacteria that help protect it from the heat. It copes with temperature changes of 40°C-90°C.

B Pompeii worms (Alvinella pompejana) live at depths of over 2 km.

1 Which of the polar bear's adaptations help it survive in its habitat?

2 Why doesn't the Pompeii worm need eyes?

Natural selection

In any habitat, there is variation between members of the same species that live there. There is **competition** between these members for resources (e.g. food, space). The members with the best adaptations will be more successful at getting the resources and more likely to survive. This is '**survival of the fittest**' or **natural selection**.

If a habitat changes, there may be individual members that, by chance, have adaptations to cope. They will survive and reproduce. The members of the species that cannot cope will die out. If all the members of a species cannot cope with a change it becomes **extinct**.

Topic B1.1: Variation

Darwin's theory

Evolution means 'a gradual change over time'. Charles Darwin (1809–1882) developed a theory of how species evolve: the theory of evolution by natural selection.

D Natural selection is often caused by environmental change.

Graph labels: Numbers of the organism that are best adapted to different conditions; Members of the population vary in their ability to cope with the conditions; 1. In these conditions most of the organisms are likely to survive; 2. If the conditions get drier, a much smaller number of the organisms are likely to survive. These organisms are known as the 'fittest'; wetter ← Conditions → drier

Darwin started thinking about evolution after noticing differences between mockingbirds on different Galapagos Islands. He thought that the birds produced more offspring than could survive and only those with better adaptations survived. So, in time, the species changed, with all members getting better adaptations as natural selection happened again and again.

If groups of the same species are separated, they may evolve differently. Darwin thought that the differences between the mockingbirds were because the mockingbirds had evolved in different conditions on the different islands.

E Española Island mockingbird

F Santiago Island mockingbird

3 Polar bears' fat layers are 7–11 cm thick. Is this continuous or discontinuous variation?

4 Define:
a evolution
b natural selection.

ResultsPlus
Watch Out!

There are different theories of evolution, not just Darwin's, so refer to 'Darwin's theory of evolution' in your exam.

Skills spotlight

In 1798, an economist called Thomas Malthus wrote an essay in which he stated that children would die of starvation if people had too many children. This helped to give Darwin an idea. How do you think Darwin was inspired by this essay to make his breakthrough?

5 State one difference between the two mockingbirds in Figures E and F.

6 Ground finches have large, powerful beaks to crush seeds. A closely related species of finch has a narrow beak, useful for probing in small holes and pulling out insect larvae. Suggest how this species could have evolved from the seed-eating species.

Learning Outcomes

1.11 Explain that organisms are adapted to their environment and that some organisms are adapted to survive in extreme environments, including deep-sea hydrothermal vents and polar regions

1.12 Demonstrate an understanding of the process of evolution by means of Darwin's theory of natural selection, including that:
a there is variation within and between species
b organisms compete for resources that are limited
c organisms best suited to the environment survive and reproduce
d organisms less well suited are unable to compete and this may lead to the extinction of the species

HSW 2 Describe the importance of creative thought in the development of hypotheses and theories

How many genes does your body contain?

B1.7 Genes

 Where is the information for variation stored?

Nearly 25 percent of all mammal species are bats! Scientists think that bats evolved from mouse-like animals about 50 million years ago. They think that a group of these animals suddenly got very long 'fingers', which they started to use as wings. The sudden change was caused by a mistake in the 'instructions' inside cells.

A *The heart-nosed bat can hear an insect walking from two metres away.*

Three of the main parts of most cells are the **cell membrane**, the **cytoplasm** and the **nucleus**. Inside the nucleus there are long strands of a substance called **DNA**. Each strand forms a structure called a **chromosome**.

1 a Draw an animal cell. Label the cell membrane, cytoplasm and nucleus.
b In which part of the cell are chromosomes found?
c What are chromosomes made of?

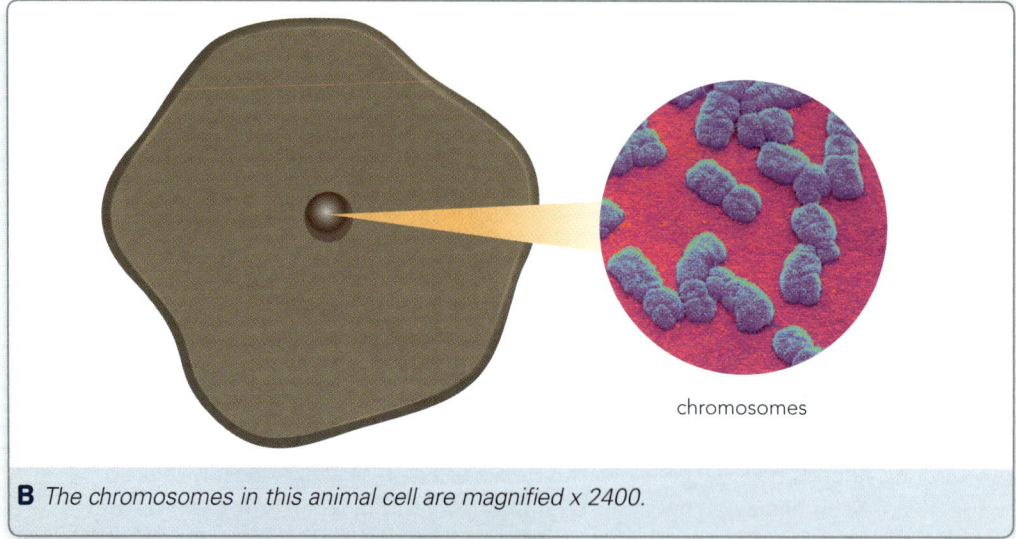

B *The chromosomes in this animal cell are magnified × 2400.*

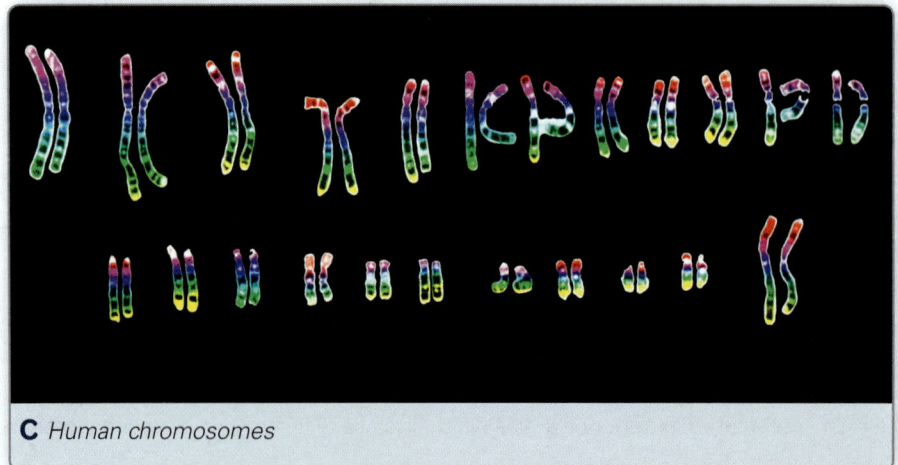

C Human chromosomes

A nucleus contains different chromosomes. There are usually two copies of each type of chromosome.

Chromosomes are divided up into **genes**. Each chromosome carries a large number of genes and each gene does a particular job. For example, many genes control variations in our characteristics – what we look like (e.g. eye colour, face shape). Variation caused by genes is **inherited variation** because we inherit our genes from our parents.

Topic B1.1: Variation

You can think of chromosomes as a set of books. Each book (chromosome) contains a set of sentences giving instructions (genes). All of the books together contain all of the instructions needed to produce a certain organism.

Alleles

Some genes for the same characteristic (e.g. eye colour) may contain slightly different instructions to create variations (e.g. brown, blue). Different forms of the same gene are called **alleles**.

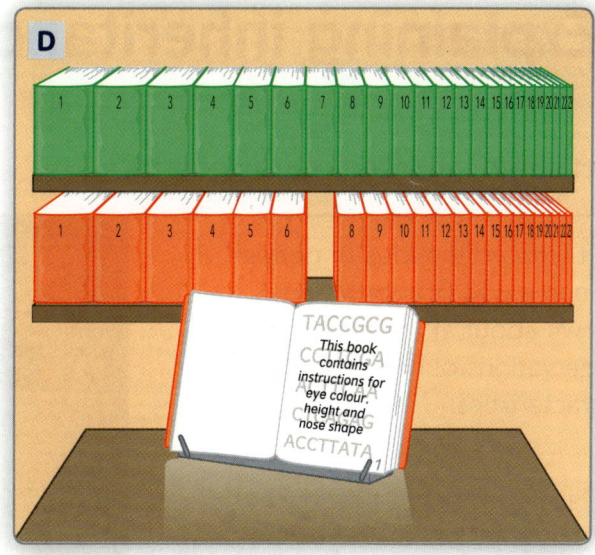

D

2 a How many chromosomes *in total* are usually found in a human body cell?
b How many pairs are there?
3 a Where are genes found?
b What do genes do?

ResultsPlus
Watch Out!

In exam questions about the differences between the same characteristic, write about alleles (and not genes).

Skills spotlight

Scientists are busy finding out what all of our alleles do. Imagine that an allele is discovered that causes a disease in older people. Someone suggests that all babies are tested for this allele. Suggest one advantage and one disadvantage of this testing.

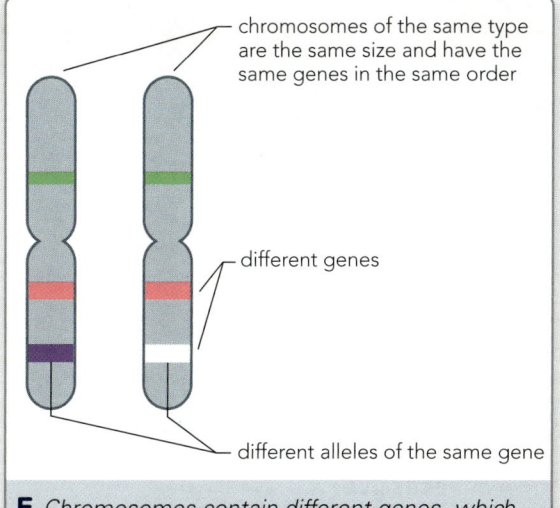

E Chromosomes contain different genes, which exist as different alleles.

Since there are two copies of every chromosome in a body cell nucleus, there are two copies of every gene. Each copy of a gene may be a different allele.

Different organisms have different numbers of chromosomes. Human body cell nuclei contain 23 pairs of chromosomes, which contain about 23 000 different genes in total. There are many alleles for each gene, so it is easy to see why each of us can inherit a different set of alleles from our parents. Each different set of alleles gives each of us slightly different characteristics.

4 What are alleles?

5 Where, inside a cell, did the mistake occur that caused some mouse-like animals to get long fingers?

6 How does the idea of alleles help us to explain why we all look different?

7 How would you add to the book analogy above to include alleles?

8 Use your knowledge of cells and genes to explain how a scientist would find out whether blood at a crime scene belongs to the victim or to a potential suspect.

Learning Outcomes

1.13 Describe the structure of the nucleus of the cell as containing chromosomes, on which genes are located

1.14 Demonstrate an understanding that genes exist in alternative forms called alleles which give rise to differences in inherited characteristics

 13 Explain how and why decisions that raise ethical issues about uses of science and technology are made

>> If you breed a pea that has purple flowers with one that has white flowers, what colour will the offspring have?

19

B1.8 Explaining inheritance

  How can we predict some inherited characteristics?

An Austrian monk first put forward the idea of genes and alleles in 1865. His name was Gregor Mendel. Chromosomes were not known about at the time, so his ideas were based on observations of how pea plants inherited discontinuous characteristics.

A *Gregor Mendel (1822–1884) grew nearly 30 000 pea plants in his investigations.*

1 How many chromosomes are in a normal human sperm cell?

Plants and animals produce **gametes** (**sex cells**). The male gametes are **sperm cells** in animals and **pollen grains** in plants. The female gametes are **ova** (or **egg cells**) in both plants and animals. Gametes are different to most body cells because they only have one copy of each chromosome.

2 Why does a pea pollen grain contain only one flower colour allele?

Gametes therefore only have one allele for each gene. In sexual reproduction two gametes fuse together. The new organism that is formed contains two alleles for each gene (one from the male parent and one from the female).

In Figure B, the offspring receives two alleles for flower colour from its parents – one white and one purple. However, only the allele for purple flowers has an effect. It is said to be **dominant**. The white flower allele has no effect if the purple flower allele is also there. This white flower allele is known as **recessive**.

Skills spotlight

The Punnett square shows scientific conventions (standard ways of doing things). Look at Figure D. Explain why the conventions used in Punnett square diagrams are useful.

ResultsPlus Watch Out!

When writing genotypes, capital letters are written before the small ones (i.e. Rr and not rR).

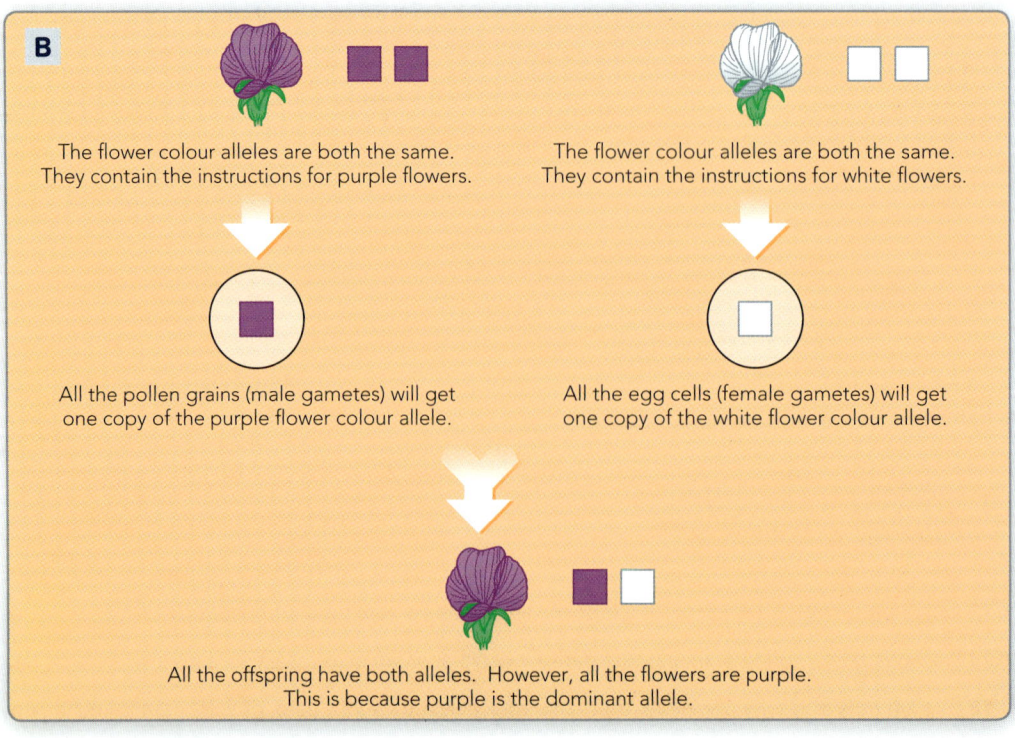

B

The flower colour alleles are both the same. They contain the instructions for purple flowers.

The flower colour alleles are both the same. They contain the instructions for white flowers.

All the pollen grains (male gametes) will get one copy of the purple flower colour allele.

All the egg cells (female gametes) will get one copy of the white flower colour allele.

All the offspring have both alleles. However, all the flowers are purple. This is because purple is the dominant allele.

A recessive characteristic is only seen if both alleles are recessive. This can be shown in a **genetic cross diagram**.

A dominant allele is shown by a capital letter (e.g. R for purple). The recessive allele has the lower case version of the *same* letter (e.g. r for *not* purple). The alleles in an organism are its **genotype**. What the organism looks like is its **phenotype**.

If both alleles for a gene in an organism are the same, the organism is **homozygous**. If they are different, it is **heterozygous**. Both parents in Figure C are heterozygous for flower colour.

C *A genetic cross diagram shows the possible combinations of alleles when two organisms breed.*

Punnett squares

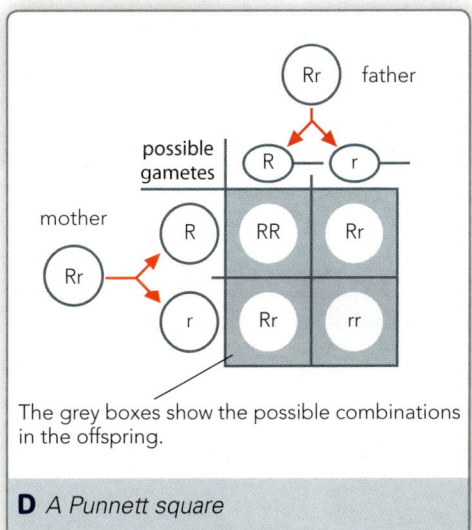

D *A Punnett square*

The possible genotypes produced when two organisms breed can also be shown in a **Punnett square**.

In Figure D there are four boxes of possible genotypes. Three boxes contain genotypes that cause the purple flower phenotype (RR and Rr). From the Punnett square you can work out the **probability** of each phenotype occurring if these plants breed.

$\frac{3}{4} = 0.75$ probability of purple

or $0.75 \times 100 = 75\%$ probability of purple

or 3:1 probability of purple

3 When will a recessive allele affect a phenotype?

Maths Skills

Probabilities can be written in three ways: as a number between 0 and 1, as a percentage or as a ratio.
- 1 or 100% means something will definitely happen.
- 0.75, 75% or 3:1 means it is quite likely to happen.
- 0 or 0% means it definitely won't happen.

4 The pea plant gene for height has two alleles: T (dominant, causing tall plants) and t (recessive, causing short plants). **a** Draw a Punnett square for breeding a homozygous short plant with a homozygous tall plant.
b What is the percentage probability of getting a tall phenotype plant?

5 Pea seeds are either yellow or green. Yellow seeds are caused by the dominant allele Y. Show how you would work out the number of the different phenotypes you would get if you crossed two heterozygous pea plants.

Learning Outcomes

1.15 Recall the meaning of, and use appropriately, the terms: dominant, recessive, homozygous, heterozygous, phenotype and genotype

1.16 Analyse and interpret patterns of inheritance using a genetic diagram, Punnett squares and family pedigrees

1.17 Calculate and analyse outcomes (using probabilities, ratios and percentages) from crosses

HSW 11 Present information using scientific conventions and symbols

Suggest a use for plastic blood cells.

B1.9 Genetic disorders

What are genetic disorders?

Professor Joseph DeSimone has developed an idea for plastic blood cells. These are tiny plastic sacs that could transport oxygen around the body. This may help people who suffer from some blood diseases.

Skills spotlight

Decisions made by the scientist who invents a new technology can affect how the technology is used. DeSimone applied for a patent on his idea. If you get a patent then other people cannot copy your idea. Why do you think scientists often patent their ideas?

One group of people who may benefit from DeSimone's research are people with **sickle-cell disease**. This is a **genetic disorder** – a disease caused by faulty alleles. The sickle-cell allele is recessive, so people need two copies of the allele to suffer from the disorder.

People with the disease easily become very tired and short of breath. Sufferers can also have times when their joints are incredibly painful because their red blood cells stick together and block blood vessels. The blocking of blood vessels can sometimes be fatal.

A Joseph DeSimone (1964–)

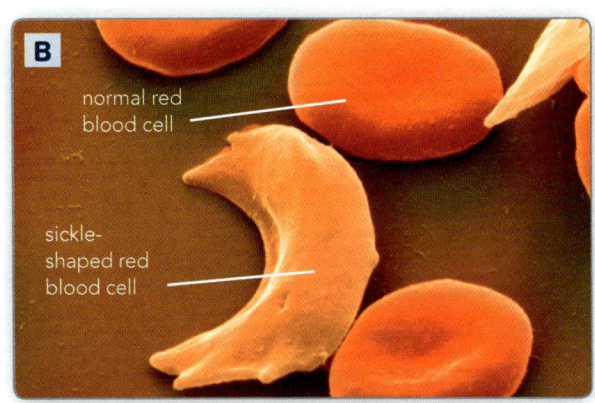

Cystic fibrosis

Another genetic disorder caused by a recessive allele is **cystic fibrosis (CF)**. In CF, the lungs get clogged with thick mucus making breathing difficult and leading to infections. Mucus also blocks some of the tubes that carry enzymes to the small intestine to digest food. Lack of enzymes can result in weight loss.

1. Why can't people catch sickle-cell disease, like catching a cold?
2. How might a person with sickle-cell disease benefit from plastic blood cells?
3. Will someone who is heterozygous for the sickle-cell allele have the disease? Explain your answer.
4. Why may CF sufferers lose weight?

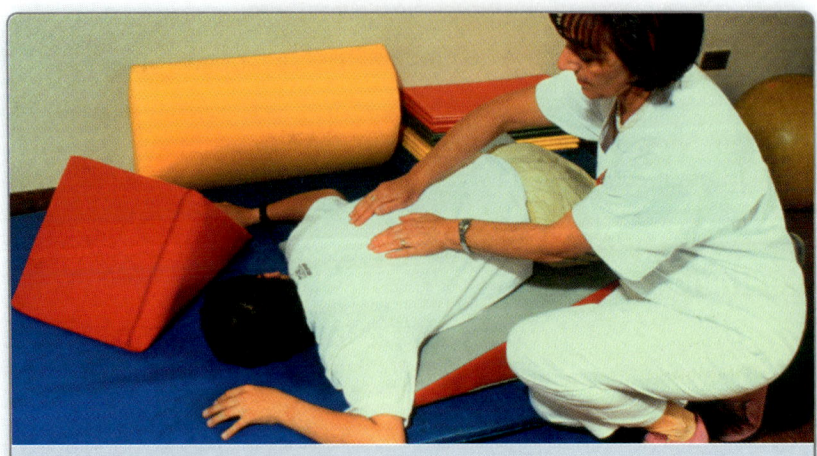

C Having the back beaten in a special way, followed by coughing, helps to clear the lungs in people with CF.

Topic B1.1: Variation

Family pedigree charts

Figure D is a **family pedigree chart**, showing how cystic fibrosis is inherited. These charts allow you to see how a genetic disorder is passed on in a family.

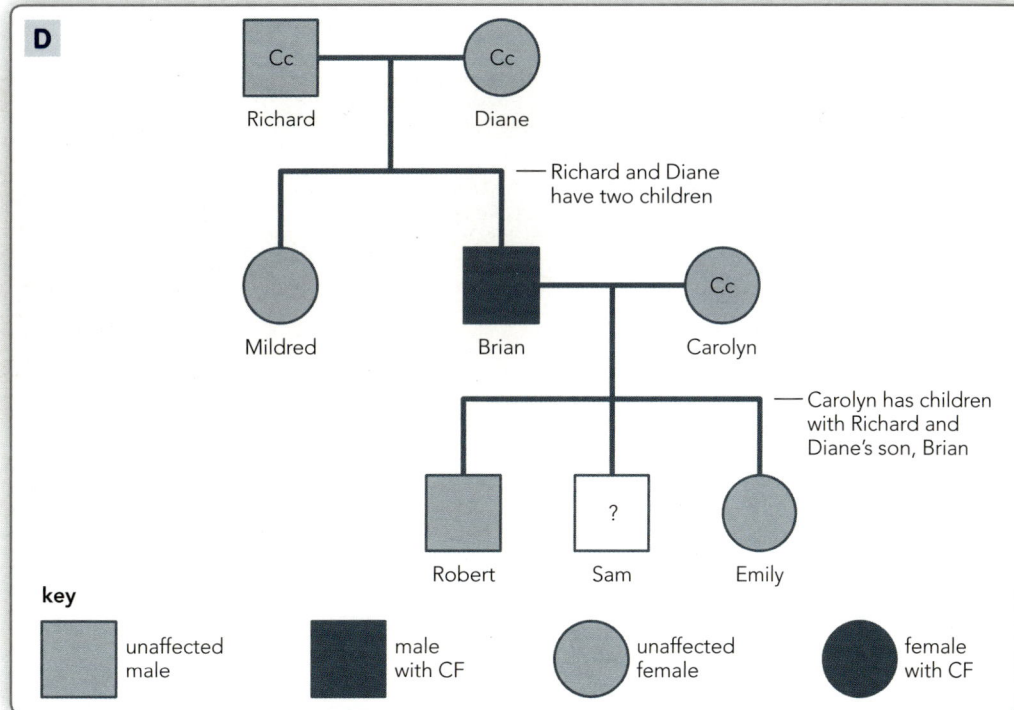

Carriers

People who inherit just one recessive allele that causes a genetic disorder are **carriers** – they don't have the disorder but can pass on the allele that causes it. Carriers of the CF allele have no symptoms of the disease because the faulty allele is recessive.

In Africa, people with sickle-cell disease usually die before they can have children, so the allele should gradually disappear from the population. However, carriers are more likely to survive a disease called **malaria** than non-carriers. They then have their own children, passing on their single copy of the sickle-cell allele. This is natural selection at work. However, the sickle-cell allele is not completely recessive, so unlike carriers of the CF allele, carriers of the sickle-cell allele may get a mild form of the disease symptoms (called 'coloured sickle-cell trait').

> **ResultsPlus**
> **Watch Out!**
> Students often lose marks by not reading the information in the key to a pedigree chart. Always study a key very carefully.

5 Look at Figure D.
a What is the recessive allele?
b What is Brian's genotype?
H c Predict how likely it is that Sam has CF.

6 State *two* symptoms of:
a cystic fibrosis
b sickle-cell disease.

H 7 Richard is a carrier of CF. What does this mean?

H 8 Would you find more or fewer people with sickle-cell disease in areas where malaria is more common? Explain your answer.

9 Doctors can check the alleles of people who are planning to have children. Suggest some reasons why couple may want to have tests like this.

Learning Outcomes

1.18 Describe the symptoms of the genetic disorders:
a sickle-cell disease
b cystic fibrosis

H 1.19 Demonstrate an understanding of the inheritance of the genetic disorders:
a sickle-cell disease
b cystic fibrosis

HSW 13 Describe the social, economic and environmental effects of decisions about the uses of science and technology

Why is your body like a house?

C1.1 The early atmosphere

What was Earth's original atmosphere like?

Figure A was taken by a space probe on the surface of Titan, one of Saturn's moons. Scientists are interested in Titan's atmosphere because they think it may be very similar to Earth's early atmosphere.

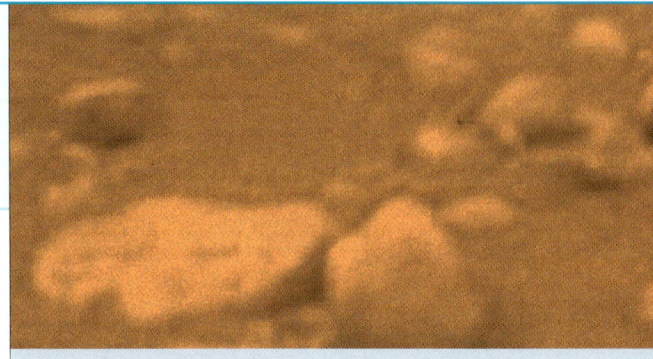

A *The surface of Titan*

The young Earth

By studying the Earth and other planets and moons, scientists hope to discover more about the Earth's early **atmosphere**.

> **1 a** Name the gases thought to have been in the Earth's early atmosphere.
> **b** What evidence supports this?
>
> **2** Some scientists believe that the Earth's early atmosphere was like that of Mars and Venus today. Explain why.
>
> **3** Some scientists believe that the Earth's early atmosphere was like that of Titan today. How is Titan's atmosphere different from that of Mars and Venus today?

As we shall see in C1.2, scientists think that the evolution of life on Earth caused its atmosphere to change. Scientists study planets and moons on which they think there is no life because these atmospheres have probably not changed for billions of years and therefore may resemble Earth's early atmosphere.

Scientists are particularly interested in volcanoes because they release large quantities of gases. Volcanoes on Earth today release mainly carbon dioxide and water vapour, along with small amounts of ammonia, methane and nitrogen. Many scientists believe that these gases would have been in our early atmosphere too. However, they cannot be certain how much of these gases early volcanoes produced.

The atmosphere of Titan is 98% nitrogen, which some scientists think was released by volcanoes. They think that the Earth's early atmosphere may have been like this.

There are also volcanoes on Mars and Venus but their atmospheres are mainly carbon dioxide. This has led other scientists to think that Earth's early atmosphere was mainly carbon dioxide.

B *Was the Earth's original atmosphere more like Titan (left) or Mars (right)?*

Recent results from space probes have shown that Titan has an icy interior rather than a rocky one (like Earth, Mars and Venus). This makes it more likely that the Earth's early atmosphere resembled that of Mars or Venus. However, this does not explain how the Earth's atmosphere later came to contain so much nitrogen. Scientists can't be certain which theory is correct.

Topic C1.1: The Earth's sea and atmosphere

Oxygen

Scientists are more certain that there was little or no oxygen in the early atmosphere on Earth. There is evidence for this idea – for example, volcanoes do not release oxygen. Also the iron compounds found in the Earth's oldest rocks are compounds that would only form in the absence of oxygen.

As the Earth became older, it cooled down. The water vapour in the hot atmosphere also cooled down, and is thought to have condensed to liquid water. This formed the oceans.

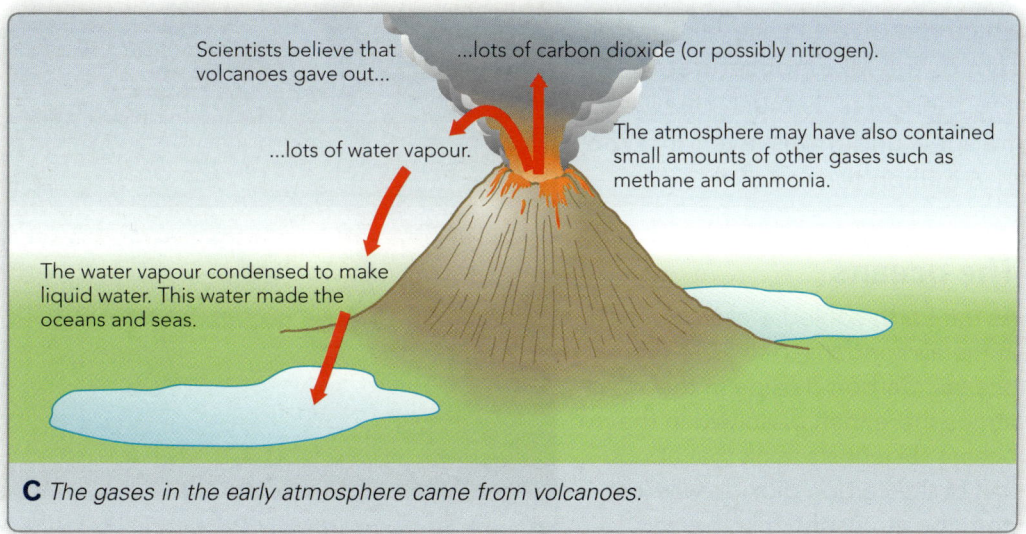

C The gases in the early atmosphere came from volcanoes.

Skills spotlight

Does the evidence that scientists have found show that the early atmosphere was mainly carbon dioxide, nitrogen or both? Explain your answer.

We have only limited evidence about the Earth's atmosphere when it was young. This means that there are uncertainties about these theories on the Earth's early atmosphere.

4 Why are scientists interested in Titan's atmosphere?

5 State two pieces of evidence that led scientists to think there was little or no oxygen in the early atmosphere.

6 Why haven't the atmospheres on Mars or Venus changed for billions of years, but the atmosphere on Earth has?

7 Describe how the oceans formed on the Earth.

ResultsPlus
Watch Out!

Some students make the mistake of saying that the early Earth's atmosphere was mainly oxygen. Remember that there was little or no oxygen in the atmosphere when the Earth was young.

Learning Outcomes

1.1 Explain that the gases produced by volcanic activity formed the Earth's early atmosphere

1.2 Recall that the early atmosphere contained: **a** little or no oxygen **b** a large amount of carbon dioxide **c** water vapour and small amounts of other gases

1.3 Explain that there are different sources of information about the development of the atmosphere which makes it difficult to be precise about the evolution of the atmosphere

1.4 Explain that condensation of water vapour formed oceans

HSW 4 Identify questions that science cannot currently answer, and explain why these questions cannot be answered

Where did the oxygen in the atmosphere come from?

C1.2 A changing atmosphere

How has the Earth's atmosphere changed?

On 21 August 1986, 1700 people died from suffocation by carbon dioxide released from Lake Nyos in Cameroon, Africa. Magma (molten rock) under the lake was releasing carbon dioxide, which dissolved in the lake water. A layer of water at the bottom of the lake got saturated with carbon dioxide, meaning there was as much dissolved as possible. More gas got trapped under this layer. In 1986, a landslide released about 1.6 million tonnes of this gas.

The oceans

As the Earth cooled, water vapour in the air condensed to form the oceans. Carbon dioxide in the atmosphere then dissolved in the oceans. Scientists think that about half of the carbon dioxide was lost from the atmosphere in this way. Some marine organisms – such as coral, molluscs and star fish – use dissolved carbon dioxide to make shells of calcium carbonate. As these creatures died, their shells fell and became sediment. Over millions of years, all these layers of sediment became **sedimentary rock**. **Limestone** is mostly calcium carbonate.

A Lake Nyos is now being 'degassed' to make it safer.

1 Limestone is a sedimentary rock. What is the main substance in limestone?

2 Much limestone is formed from the shells of marine organisms. Why do marine organisms with shells remove carbon dioxide from the atmosphere?

B You can sometimes find shells in limestone because that's how it has formed.

Photosynthesis

Scientists believe that life started on Earth about 4 billion years ago. About 1 billion years ago, some organisms developed the ability to **photosynthesise**, taking in carbon dioxide and releasing oxygen.

Over time, more photosynthesising organisms evolved, including plants. Increasing levels of photosynthesis sped up the rate at which carbon dioxide was removed from the atmosphere and the rate at which oxygen was added.

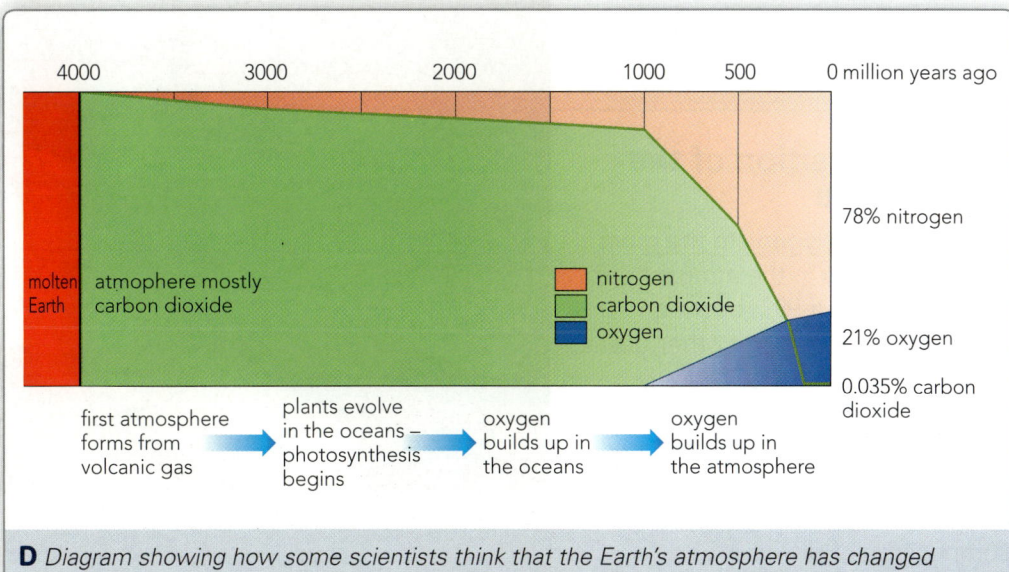

C These sedimentary structures are called 'stromatolites'. Some are well over 2 billion years old and contain fossils of simple organisms that released oxygen.

D Diagram showing how some scientists think that the Earth's atmosphere has changed

3 Which two of the following removed carbon dioxide from the early atmosphere?
a respiration
b photosynthesis
c dissolving in oceans
d burning fuels

4 Explain how the amount of oxygen in the atmosphere gradually increased.

5 There are different theories about the Earth's early atmosphere (see C1.1). Look back and decide which theory the scientists who prepared Figure D support.

6 Explain how carbon dioxide from the early atmosphere ended up in sedimentary rocks.

ResultsPlus
Watch Out!

In exams, some students write that photosynthesis releases nitrogen. Remember that photosynthesis uses up carbon dioxide and releases oxygen.

Learning Outcomes

1.5 Describe how the amount of carbon dioxide in the atmosphere was reduced by: **a** the dissolution of carbon dioxide into the oceans **b** the later incorporation of this dissolved carbon dioxide into marine organisms which eventually formed carbonate rocks

1.6 Explain that the growth of primitive plants used carbon dioxide and released oxygen by photosynthesis and consequently the amount of oxygen in the atmosphere gradually increased

HSW 3 Describe how phenomena are explained using scientific theories and ideas

Can you remove oxygen from the air? 27

C1.4 The atmosphere today

What is the atmosphere like now?

Oxygen bars are very popular in Japan. They are often found in cities with polluted air. Customers breathe in air with a high concentration of oxygen for a few minutes. People find the experience relaxing and refreshing.

A Relaxing in an oxygen bar

The composition of the atmosphere

Nitrogen and oxygen are the most abundant gases in the atmosphere, making up about 99% between them. Small amounts of other gases make up the other 1%. There is also water vapour present in the atmosphere. The amount of water vapour changes from day to day and so it is not included when giving the composition of dry air.

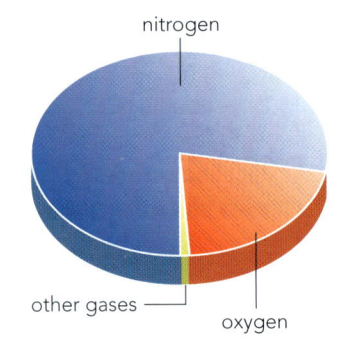

Gas	Formula	% in dry air
nitrogen	N_2	78
oxygen	O_2	21
argon	Ar	0.9
carbon dioxide	CO_2	0.04
other gases		traces

B The gases in dry air

Some of the other 1% of gases in the atmosphere are unreactive **noble gases**, mainly argon. A small amount of carbon dioxide is also found. There are also **trace** amounts of other gases in the atmosphere including carbon monoxide, methane, nitrogen oxides and sulfur dioxide.

The amounts of these gases in the atmosphere can vary. Some of the changes in the amounts of these gases have natural causes. For example, volcanoes can release a lot of sulfur dioxide and lightning can produce nitrogen oxides.

Other changes in the amounts of these gases are caused by human activities. **Deforestation** means that there are fewer trees to remove carbon dioxide from the atmosphere by photosynthesis. Burning fossil fuels increases the amounts of carbon dioxide, carbon monoxide and sulfur dioxide in the atmosphere. Engines and furnaces can release nitrogen oxides. Cattle and rice fields release large quantities of methane.

Some of these gases are harmful to people and/or the environment. It is important that scientists monitor how much of these gases are in air.

1 a List the three main gases in air, in order of abundance. Put the most abundant gas first.
b Draw a bar chart to show the three most abundant gases in the air.

Topic C1.1: The Earth's sea and atmosphere

This jungle is being cleared for timber and to make farmland. Burning the jungle produces carbon dioxide, and also means that there are fewer trees to remove carbon dioxide from the atmosphere.

The cattle that live on the cleared land release a lot of methane as they digest their food.

C Deforestation is changing the atmosphere.

Skills spotlight

The concentration of carbon dioxide in the atmosphere can change because of natural processes and also through human activity. Suggest how scientists could measure how global levels of carbon dioxide are changing. Then explain why it is important that scientists from different places share their results.

Formation of nitrogen

Nitrogen is the main gas in the atmosphere today. It makes up 78% of the air. There are different theories about where it has come from.

One theory is that volcanoes released nitrogen when the Earth was young – this means that the atmosphere has always contained a lot of nitrogen. Another theory is that most of the nitrogen was added to the atmosphere gradually due to the reactions of nitrogen-containing compounds released from volcanoes.

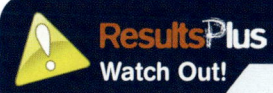

ResultsPlus Watch Out!

Some students wrongly think that there is a lot of hydrogen in the air when, in fact, there is hardly any.

2 Give one example of a natural activity that could increase the amount of these gases in the atmosphere:
a sulfur dioxide **b** nitrogen oxides **c** methane.

3 a Give two examples of human activities that could increase the amount of carbon dioxide in the atmosphere.
b Many of the trees removed by deforestation are burned. Give two reasons why deforestation increases the amount of carbon dioxide in the atmosphere.

4 Small changes happen in the composition of the Earth's atmosphere. Describe how some of these changes are caused by natural and human activities.

Learning Outcomes

1.8 Describe the current composition of the atmosphere and interpret data sources showing this information

1.9 Demonstrate an understanding of how small changes in the atmosphere occur through: **a** volcanic activity **b** human activity, including the burning of fossil fuels, farming and deforestation

HSW 14 Describe how scientists share data and discuss new ideas, and how over time this process helps to reduce uncertainties and revise scientific theories

How can footsteps be preserved for millions of years?

C1.5 Rocks and their formation

How are different rocks formed?

In 1978, scientists working in Tanzania excavated a trail of fossilised footprints from our ancestors – creatures that lived 3.6 million years ago. They had walked through a layer of ash from a volcano. This was later covered by more layers of ash, preserving the footprints. The layers gradually became harder and eventually they turned into rock. More recently, erosion revealed some of the prints.

A Fossilised footprints of two adults and a child

B Granite has large crystals of different colours.

Igneous rocks

Rocks deep inside the Earth may become hot enough to partially melt. Molten rock is called **magma**. It may stay inside the Earth, or it may erupt onto the surface as **lava**. When molten rock cools down it **solidifies** and becomes solid rock. Rocks formed this way are called **igneous rocks**. They contain crystals that interlock.

The size of the **crystals** depends on the **rate** at which the magma or lava cools. The slower it cools, the larger the crystals. For example, **granite** forms from magma that cools slowly deep below the surface of the Earth. It has large crystals, whereas igneous rocks that cool quickly have small crystals.

1 Explain how you know that granite forms from magma that cools slowly.

Sedimentary rocks

Rocks are broken into smaller pieces by physical processes, such as the expansion of water when it freezes. They are also broken up by chemical reactions with water or air. **Erosion** happens when these pieces of rock are transported – for example in a river. Rivers carry large amounts of broken rock towards the sea, where it may become **sedimentary rock**.

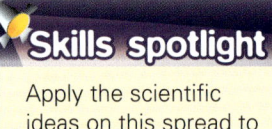

Skills spotlight

Apply the scientific ideas on this spread to explain the difference in crystal size between granite and rhyolite, and to suggest where each rock may have formed.

C Rhyolite has a similar chemical composition to granite. Its crystals are too small to see with the naked eye.

Most sedimentary rocks form from pieces of other rocks. Others form from the hard parts of dead organisms. **Chalk** and **limestone**, which are mostly calcium carbonate, can be formed from sea shells. Layers of this **sediment** build up on the sea bed. Over a long time, these layers are compacted, or squashed together, to form rock. Sedimentary rocks may contain the **fossil** remains of dead plants and animals, or imprints such as footmarks.

Topic C1.2: Materials from the Earth

Metamorphic rocks

The action of heat and/or pressure can change rocks, causing new crystals to form. The changed rocks are called **metamorphic rocks**. For example, **marble** is a metamorphic rock formed from chalk or limestone. The grains in chalk and limestone are weakly joined together with small gaps between them. When marble forms, these grains become new crystals of calcium carbonate that interlock tightly. This makes marble harder than chalk or limestone.

D Marble is a metamorphic rock formed by the action of heat and pressure.

Erosion

Sedimentary rocks are more susceptible to erosion than igneous rocks or metamorphic rocks. This is because metamorphic rocks and igneous rocks have interlocking crystals. They are harder and less easily eroded than sedimentary rocks.

F Salisbury Crags in Scotland are made of igneous rocks exposed by the erosion of other rock.

E Mylonite is a metamorphic rock formed mainly by the action of pressure alone.

2 Explain what type of rock is most likely to have been eroded to produce the crags in Figure F.

3 a Name the main compound in chalk and limestone.
b Explain why the same compound is found in marble.

4 Name one example of each of the following types of rock, and describe each type: **a** igneous rock **b** metamorphic rock **c** sedimentary rock.

5 Suggest why fossils are often found in sedimentary rocks but not in igneous rocks.

6 Describe how an igneous rock may become a sedimentary rock, which in turn may become a metamorphic rock. Explain what must happen for the metamorphic rock to become an igneous rock.

ResultsPlus Watch Out!

In exams, some students write that metamorphic rocks form when other rocks melt. Metamorphic rocks can form from rock that has been heated – but not strongly enough to melt it.

Learning Outcomes

2.1 Describe that igneous rocks, such as granite, are: **a** formed by the solidification of magma or lava **b** made of crystals whose size depends on the rate of cooling

2.2 Describe chalk and limestone as examples of sedimentary rocks

2.3 Describe how sedimentary rocks are formed by the compaction of layers of sediment over a very long time period

2.4 Recall that sedimentary rocks: **a** may contain fossils **b** are susceptible to erosion

2.5 Describe marble as an example of a metamorphic rock

2.6 Describe the formation of metamorphic rocks by the action of heat and/or pressure, including the formation of marble from chalk or limestone

2.7 Recall that limestone, chalk and marble exist in the Earth's crust and that they are all natural forms of calcium carbonate

HSW 3 Describe how phenomena are explained using scientific theories and ideas

Is limestone of any use to us?

C1.6 Limestone and its uses

 What do cement, concrete and glass have in common?

Around 76 million tonnes of limestone are quarried in the UK every year. This is more than one tonne of the rock for each person in the UK. What uses are there for all this limestone?

Using limestone

Limestone is cut into blocks to be used for constructing buildings. It is also crushed into smaller lumps to be used to make a firm base for railway lines and roads. Limestone is a raw material for the manufacture of cement, concrete and glass. Figure B shows how much is used for each purpose.

A A limestone quarry in Scotland

> 1 What is the best way to present the information in Figure B and why?
>
> 2 What is the biggest use of limestone?

Use	Percentage (%)
Construction	57
Making concrete and cement	22
Other uses, e.g. making glass	16
Making steel and iron alloys	5

B The main uses of limestone

Quarrying limestone

Limestone is removed from the ground at a **quarry**. Explosives are used to break the limestone into pieces. These are cut or crushed into useful sizes, then taken by road or rail to the customers.

Limestone is an important material and there is a commercial need for it but quarries have benefits and drawbacks. They are in the countryside, where jobs may be difficult to find. Having jobs at a quarry helps local families and businesses. Limestone is valuable and is exported to other countries, helping the (UK's) economy.

Unfortunately, quarries are commonly in attractive places like the Peak District. They are dusty and noisy. Quarries may affect the quality of life for local people and damage the tourist industry. Heavy lorries cause extra traffic, noise and pollution. Land taken up by a quarry cannot be used for farming or other purposes. Quarries destroy the original landscape. However, the quarry owners usually restore it later, often as farmland or a nature reserve.

> **ResultsPlus Watch Out!**
>
> If you have to evaluate the advantages of opening a new quarry, make sure you include arguments both for and against it. You may not gain full marks if you only discuss one side of the argument.

Thermal decomposition

Limestone, chalk and marble are natural sources of calcium carbonate. When it is heated strongly, calcium carbonate breaks down (decomposes) to form calcium oxide and carbon dioxide. **Word equations** show what happens in chemical reactions. This is the word equation for calcium carbonate decomposing:

calcium carbonate → calcium oxide + carbon dioxide

This type of reaction is called **thermal decomposition**. Thermal decomposition of limestone is used in the manufacture of cement and glass.

Making cement and concrete

Cement is made by heating limestone with powdered clay. Cement is an ingredient in mortar – the mixture used by bricklayers to hold bricks together in walls. **Concrete** is made by mixing cement with sand, gravel and water. Concrete is widely used in the construction of buildings and bridges.

> **Skills spotlight**
>
> Design a questionnaire that could be used to discover the views of local people as to whether a new quarry should be opened. How would you collect both qualitative and quantitative information from your questionnaire?

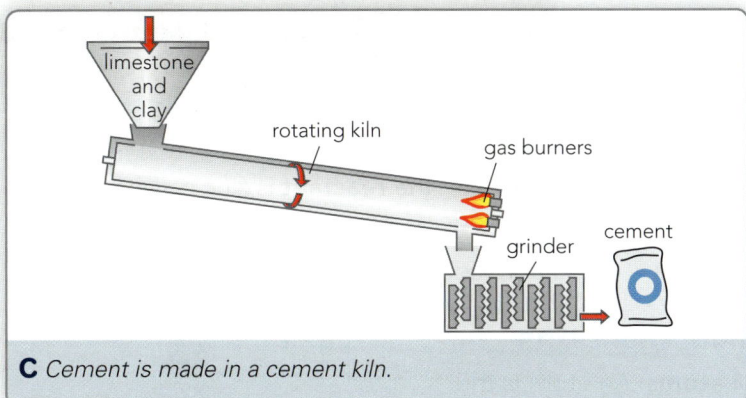

C Cement is made in a cement kiln.

Glass is made by heating limestone with sand and sodium carbonate. A chemical reaction occurs and liquid glass is made. This cools to form the hard, transparent solid we use for making windows.

D Glass bottles being made from molten glass

3 Write a word equation for the thermal decomposition of calcium carbonate.

4 Describe how each of the following is made:
a cement b concrete c glass.

5 Draw a table or spider diagram to show the advantages and disadvantages of quarrying limestone.

6 Explain why an increase in demand for new housing may cause an increase in demand for limestone.

Learning Outcomes

2.8 Demonstrate an understanding of the balance between the demand for limestone and the economic, environmental and social effects of quarrying it

2.9 Demonstrate an understanding of the commercial need for quarrying calcium carbonate on a large scale, as a raw material, for the formation of glass, cement and concrete

2.10 Describe the thermal decomposition of calcium carbonate into calcium oxide and carbon dioxide

HSW 10 Use qualitative and quantitative approaches when presenting scientific ideas and arguments, and recording observations

Do other carbonates break down when heated?

C1.8 Chemical reaction

 What happens to the atoms during chemical reactions?

Zinc carbonate is used as a fireproof ingredient of some plastics. In a fire, the zinc carbonate absorbs some of the heat. As it decomposes, it releases carbon dioxide. This helps to reduce the amount of oxygen available near the surface of the burning plastic. The zinc oxide left behind helps to form a layer of heat-resistant material. Zinc carbonate is chosen instead of calcium carbonate because it decomposes more easily when it is heated.

A *Fireproof materials help to protect firefighters.*

Word equations

Word equations show what happens in chemical reactions. In general:

reactants → products

In the thermal decomposition of zinc carbonate, the **reactant** is zinc carbonate. The **products** are zinc oxide and carbon dioxide. Here is the word equation:

zinc carbonate → zinc oxide + carbon dioxide

Atoms and chemical reactions

Substances are made of **atoms**. An atom is the smallest part of an **element** that can take part in chemical reactions. A **compound** consists of the atoms of two or more different elements chemically joined together. The **chemical formula** of a compound shows the symbols of the elements it contains and the ratios in which their atoms are present.

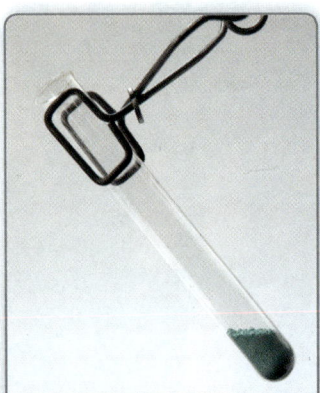

B *Green copper carbonate decomposes very easily when it is heated – it forms black copper oxide and carbon dioxide.*

In all chemical reactions, the atoms of the reactants rearrange to form new products. None of the atoms are destroyed in the reaction, and no new ones are formed. The products have different physical and chemical properties from those of the reactants because their atoms are combined differently.

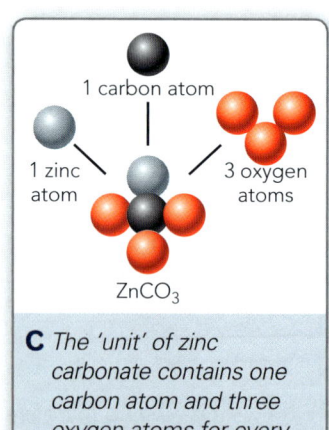

C *The 'unit' of zinc carbonate contains one carbon atom and three oxygen atoms for every zinc atom. So its chemical formula is $ZnCO_3$.*

1 Write the word equation for the thermal decomposition of copper carbonate.

2 What is an atom?

3 The formula for calcium carbonate is $CaCO_3$.
a How many different elements does calcium carbonate contain?
b What does the '3' in the formula tell you?

Balanced equations

Balanced equations show what happens to the atoms in a chemical reaction. Here is the balanced equation for the thermal decomposition of zinc carbonate:

zinc carbonate → zinc oxide + carbon dioxide
$ZnCO_3(s)$ → $ZnO(s)$ + $CO_2(g)$

There is one Zn, one C and three O on each side of the equation. Each of these symbols represents an atom of an element. There are the same numbers of atoms of each element on both sides, so it is a *balanced* equation.

The symbols (s) and (g) are **state symbols**. They show that $ZnCO_3$ and ZnO are solids, and CO_2 is a gas. Pure liquids are shown by (l). **Aqueous solutions**, formed when substances dissolve in water, are shown by (aq).

Conserving mass

Atoms are not made or destroyed in a chemical reaction – they are only rearranged. So the total mass before and after a reaction is the same. This works for all reactions. It is easiest to demonstrate in reactions where none of the reactants or products are allowed to leave the system. This happens if the reaction takes place in a stoppered test tube, or in a solution where none of the substances leave the liquid.

Precipitation reactions

Precipitation reactions happen when soluble substances react together to form an **insoluble** product, called the **precipitate**. For example, silver nitrate and potassium bromide are soluble.
Their solutions react together to form insoluble cream-coloured silver bromide:

silver nitrate + potassium bromide → potassium nitrate + silver bromide

$AgNO_3(aq)$ + $KBr(aq)$ → $KNO_3(aq)$ + $AgBr(s)$

> 5 A student mixes 2 g of a lead nitrate solution with 2 g of a potassium iodide solution. A precipitation reaction occurs. What is the total mass of the mixture after the reaction?
>
> 6 When 10.0 g of calcium carbonate is heated strongly, it decomposes completely to form 5.6 g of calcium oxide. What mass of carbon dioxide must have been released?
>
> 7 The table shows temperatures at which different carbonates decompose:
>
> | Carbonate | Temperature (°C) |
> |---|---|
> | calcium carbonate | 825 |
> | copper carbonate | 200 |
> | sodium carbonate | 1000 |
> | zinc carbonate | 300 |
>
> Use this information to put the carbonates in order of ease of decomposition – start with the one that is most difficult to decompose.

H 4 Write a balanced equation for the thermal decomposition of calcium carbonate to calcium oxide, CaO, and carbon dioxide, CO_2.

Skills spotlight

H Describe the advantages and disadvantages of using balanced equations rather than word equations.

ResultsPlus Watch Out!

H Students often forget or mix up state symbols. NaCl(aq) means an aqueous solution of sodium chloride, but NaCl(l) means molten or liquid sodium chloride.

Learning Outcomes

2.12 Describe the ease of thermal decomposition of different metal carbonates

2.13 Demonstrate an understanding that: **a** atoms are the smallest particles of an element that can take part in chemical reactions **b** during chemical reactions, atoms are neither created nor destroyed **c** during chemical reactions, atoms are rearranged to make new products with different properties from the reactants

2.16 Demonstrate an understanding that the total mass before and after a reaction in a sealed container is unchanged, as shown practically by a precipitation reaction

HSW 11 Present information using scientific conventions and symbols

Why is building dams hot work?

C1.9 Reactions of calcium compounds

 How does calcium carbonate react with other substances?

Concrete releases heat as it sets. The Hoover Dam was built in the USA in 1936 and so much concrete was used that it would have taken 125 years to cool down! To speed this up, cooling water was passed through pipes set in the surrounding concrete to help to cool the setting concrete.

A The Hoover Dam contains over $3\,300\,000\,m^3$ of concrete.

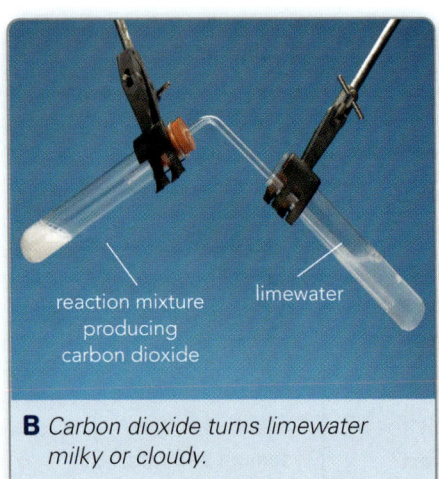

B Carbon dioxide turns limewater milky or cloudy.

Making limewater

Limestone is a raw material used in the manufacture of concrete. When limestone is heated, the calcium carbonate that it contains forms calcium oxide.

calcium carbonate → calcium oxide + carbon dioxide

$CaCO_3(s) → CaO(s) + CO_2(g)$

A vigorous reaction happens when water is added to calcium oxide. A lot of heat is released, which makes the water boil as it touches the calcium oxide. Calcium hydroxide, a crumbly white solid, forms in the reaction:

calcium oxide + water → calcium hydroxide

$CaO(s) + H_2O(l) → Ca(OH)_2(s)$

Calcium hydroxide dissolves when more water is added, forming calcium hydroxide solution. This solution is often called **limewater**.

The brackets in the formula $Ca(OH)_2$ show that each 'unit' of calcium hydroxide contains two hydroxide 'units'. So a 'unit' of calcium hydroxide contains one calcium atom, two oxygen atoms and two hydrogen atoms.

A test for carbon dioxide

Limewater turns cloudy (milky) in the presence of carbon dioxide. This is because white insoluble calcium carbonate forms:

calcium hydroxide + carbon dioxide → calcium carbonate + water

$Ca(OH)_2(aq) + CO_2(g) → CaCO_3(s) + H_2O(l)$

ResultsPlus Watch Out!

Remember that atoms are not used up in chemical reactions. They are rearranged to make new products instead.

1 Name the precipitate made when carbon dioxide reacts with limewater.

Topic C1.2: Materials from the Earth

If a lot of carbon dioxide is bubbled through the limewater, the calcium carbonate disappears and a colourless solution is formed. This happens because carbon dioxide dissolves in water to form an acidic solution, which reacts with the calcium carbonate. Other acids react with calcium carbonate, which is useful for farmers and coal-fired power stations.

Neutralising acids with limestone

Acids are neutralised by alkalis. This is called a **neutralisation** reaction. Calcium carbonate, calcium oxide and calcium hydroxide can neutralise acids. Some crops do not grow well if the soil is too acidic. Farmers may need to reduce the acidity of their soil. They spray powdered calcium carbonate, calcium oxide or calcium hydroxide over their fields to do this.

Many power stations burn coal. Coal naturally contains sulfur and sulfur compounds. When the coal burns, the sulfur forms sulfur dioxide:

sulfur + oxygen → sulfur dioxide
H $S(s)$ + $O_2(g)$ → $SO_2(g)$

Nitrogen oxides are also formed when the coal burns. Sulfur dioxide and nitrogen oxides are acidic gases. They produce acid rain if they escape from the chimneys into the atmosphere. To stop this happening, wet powdered calcium carbonate is sprayed through the waste gases. This reacts with the acidic gases and neutralises them. In this way, limestone reduces harmful emissions and helps to reduce acid rain.

> **Skills spotlight**
> Outline how you could test the idea that the mass of calcium oxide obtained by thermal decomposition is directly proportional to the mass of calcium carbonate heated. What would you do? How would you analyse the results?

> 2 Describe what happens when water is added to calcium oxide.
>
> 3 a State the common name for the solution formed when calcium hydroxide dissolves in water.
> b Describe a laboratory test for carbon dioxide using this solution.
>
> 4 Calcium carbonate breaks down to form calcium oxide and carbon dioxide when heated. Calcium oxide reacts with water to form calcium hydroxide. This reacts with carbon dioxide to form calcium carbonate again, and water.
> Write equations to describe these three reactions.
>
> 5 Which calcium compounds can be used to reduce soil acidity?
> a Explain how they reduce the acidity.
> b Explain why farmers need to control soil acidity.

> 6 Describe the use of calcium carbonate in reducing harmful emissions from coal-fired power stations.

Learning Outcomes

2.14 Describe the effect of water on calcium oxide

2.15 Explain that calcium hydroxide dissolves in water to form a solution, known as limewater

2.17 Explain how calcium oxide, calcium hydroxide and calcium carbonate can be used to neutralise soil acidity

2.18 Explain how calcium carbonate can be used to remove acidic gases from coal-fired power station chimneys, reducing harmful emissions and helping to reduce acid rain

HSW 5 Plan to test a scientific idea, answer a scientific question, or solve a scientific problem by selecting appropriate data to test a hypothesis

Why would eating chalk be helpful for an upset stomach?

P1.1 The Solar System

 How do we know what is in the Universe?

Ancient cultures from all over the world made up stories about the stars and planets. They also used our closest star (the Sun) to tell the time.

A *Twice a year, the Pyramid of Kukulcan creates shadows that look like a giant snake. The snake was an important symbol to the Mayan people who built the pyramid over 1000 years ago.* Shadows form a snake on the two days in a year when the length of night is equal to the length of daylight.

1 What is a geocentric model?

ResultsPlus Watch Out!

Students often confuse the names *geocentric* (Earth-centred) and *heliocentric* (Sun-centred) for ideas about the Solar System. Make sure you learn the difference between them.

Like the ancient Mayans in Central America, the ancient Greeks made detailed measurements of the movements of objects in the sky. The Greek astronomer Ptolemy (c. 90–168) used these measurements to explain how the Sun, the Moon and the planets moved in **orbits**. His idea put the Earth in the centre of everything – a **geocentric** model.

The Polish astronomer Nicolaus Copernicus (1473–1543) thought that Ptolemy's measurements fitted a different model – a model with the Sun at the centre of the Solar System. The Church did not like this **heliocentric** model and a priest inserted an introduction into Copernicus's book before it was published saying that the book contained ideas with no proof.

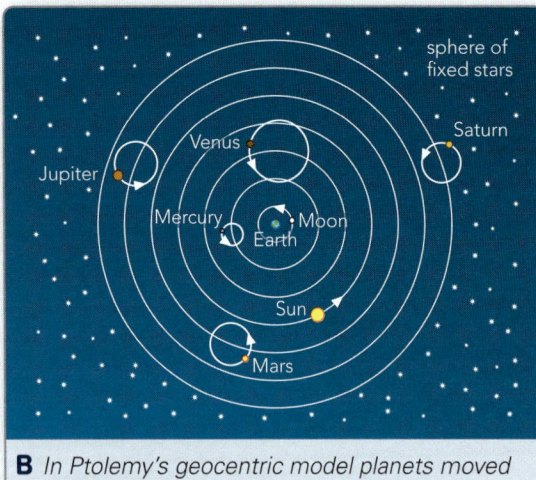

B *In Ptolemy's geocentric model planets moved in small circles as they orbited the Earth.*

C *Copernicus's heliocentric model of the Solar System*

The **telescope** was invented at the end of the 16th century. It allowed scientists to see objects in space in much greater detail than with the **naked eye**, and to find new objects.

Using a telescope, the Italian astronomer Galileo Galilei (1564–1642) discovered four of Jupiter's moons. By plotting their movements he showed that not everything orbited the Earth. This and other observations led him to support Copernicus's idea. However, the Church was still against the idea, and Galileo was put under house arrest for the last 10 years of his life.

Topic P1.1: Visible light and the Solar System

> **2 a** Describe two differences between Ptolemy's and Copernicus's models.
> **b** Describe two similarities between the two models.
> **c** Suggest one way in which our current model of the Solar System is different from Copernicus's.
>
> **3** How do Galileo's observations of Jupiter's moons support Copernicus's theory?

As telescopes improved, so more discoveries were made, including the planets Uranus and Neptune, and the dwarf planet Pluto.

Astronomy today

Luminous objects in space give out **visible light** that travels as waves of energy. These visible **light waves** allow people to study distant objects. The invention of photography has allowed astronomers to make more detailed observations than they could by just making drawings.

Many objects in space do not give out much visible light but give out other types of energy-carrying waves, like **radio waves** and **microwaves**. Today, different types of telescopes are used to detect these different types of waves and scientists analyse the data collected to make conclusions about the Universe.

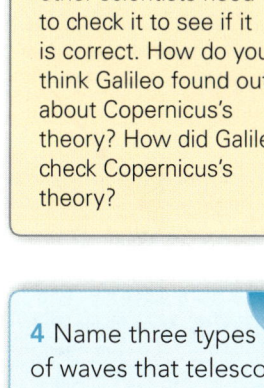

Skills spotlight

When someone proposes a new theory, other scientists need to check it to see if it is correct. How do you think Galileo found out about Copernicus's theory? How did Galileo check Copernicus's theory?

D The Planck space telescope detects microwaves.

> **4** Name three types of waves that telescopes can detect.
>
> **5** Suggest one reason why modern telescopes are put into space.
>
> **6** Describe how our understanding of the Universe has changed over time because of changes in technology.

Learning Outcomes

1.1 Describe how ideas about the structure of the Solar System have changed over time, including the change from the geocentric to the heliocentric models and the discovery of new planets

1.2 Demonstrate an understanding of how scientists use waves to find out information about our Universe, including:
  a the Solar System **b** the Milky Way

1.3 Discuss how Galileo's observations of Jupiter, using the telescope, provided evidence for the heliocentric model of the solar system

1.4 Compare methods of observing the Universe using visible light, including the naked-eye, photography and telescopes

HSW 14 Describe how scientists share data and discuss new ideas, and how over time this process helps to reduce uncertainties and revise scientific theories

Why does a telescope have two lenses?

P1.2 Refracting telescopes

 How can telescopes make faraway objects appear larger?

One of the first people to observe the night sky with a telescope was an English mathematician called Thomas Harriot (1560–1621). The telescope allowed him to see the Moon in much greater detail, and he made the first drawings of its craters.

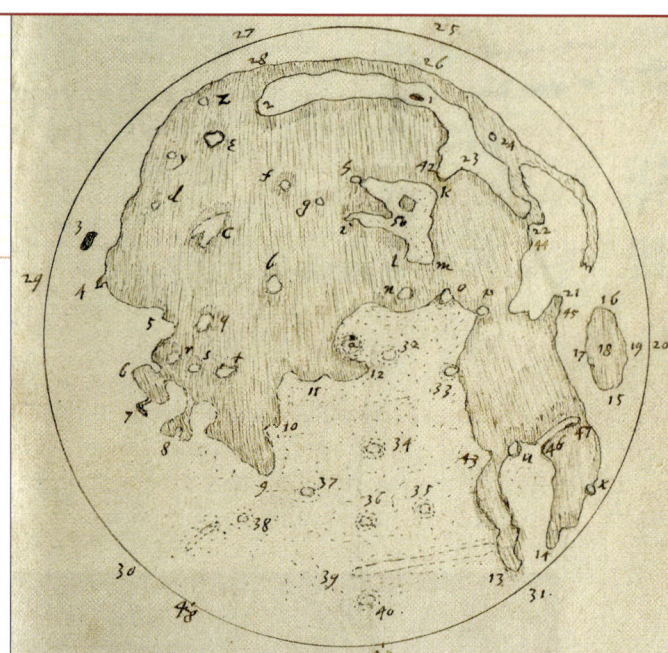

A Thomas Harriot's earliest Moon drawing from 1609.

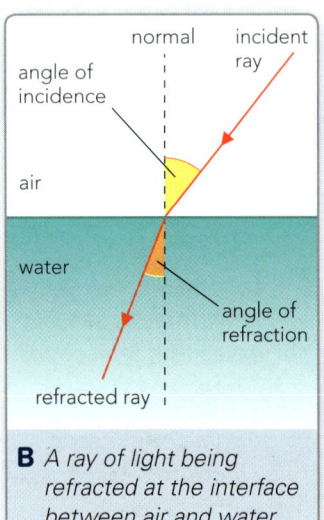

B A ray of light being refracted at the interface between air and water

Refraction

Light travels in straight lines. However, it can change direction when it moves into a different material. The change in direction is called **refraction** and happens at the **interface** (boundary) between the two materials. Figure B shows an example of this when light moves from air into water. A line at right angles to the interface is called the **normal** line.

Refraction in lenses

A **lens** is a transparent block that has been shaped so that its interface changes the directions of parallel light waves.

A **converging lens** is a glass block that is curved on both sides to make it thicker in the middle. Light rays entering a lens from air are brought together or **converge**. Rays of light from distant objects are almost parallel when they reach us. A convex lens focuses these rays. The distance between the focus and the lens is called the **focal length** of that lens. The focal length of a converging lens can be found by focusing the **image** of a distant object onto a piece of paper.

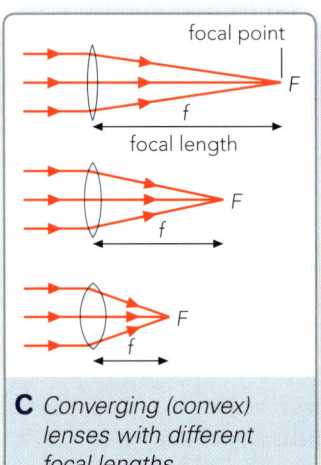

C Converging (convex) lenses with different focal lengths

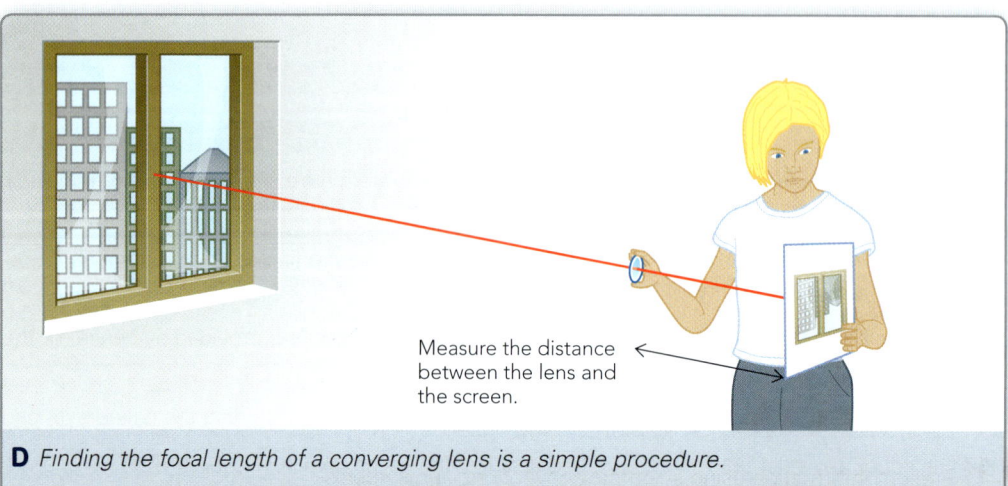

D Finding the focal length of a converging lens is a simple procedure.

1 Give examples of two different materials.

2 Write a short definition of 'refraction'.

In a **refracting telescope**, a convex lens (the **objective lens**) creates an image inside the tube and another lens (the **eyepiece lens**) is used to **magnify** this image.

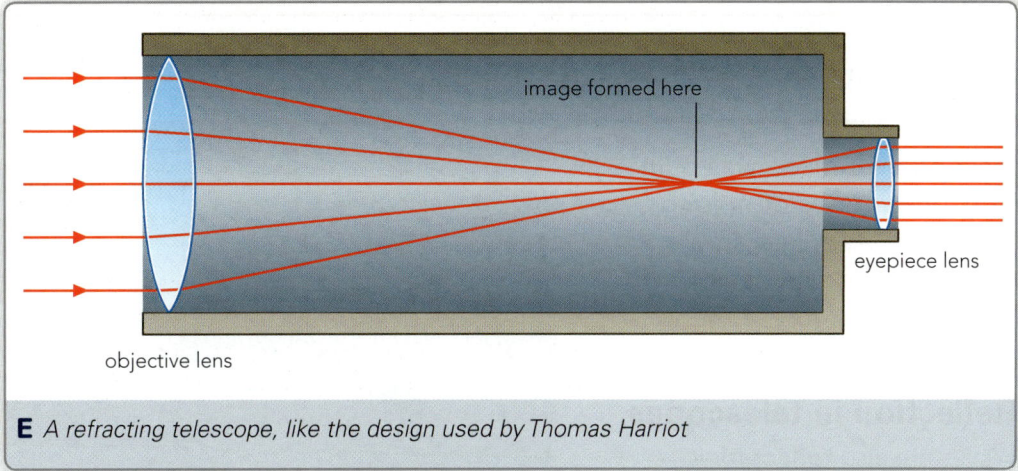

E *A refracting telescope, like the design used by Thomas Harriot*

3 What does 'focal length' mean?

4 How can you measure the focal length of a convex lens?

Scientists use conventions (standard ways of doing things) in diagrams to help them to explain how things work. Describe two conventions that are used in the diagrams on these two pages.

F *Waves change speed at an interface, so they change direction.*

Refraction occurs because light travels at different speeds in different materials. Figure F shows how this causes the change in direction. Moving from air to glass, light slows down and refracts towards the normal. For light waves travelling in the opposite direction, the opposite change in speed occurs.

ResultsPlus Watch Out!

When you draw light rays, they must be straight (use a ruler!) and should have arrows on the lines to show their direction.

H 5 Describe what would happen if a light ray travelling inside a glass block entered a material where the speed was:
a greater than inside the glass b less than inside the glass.

6 Describe the difference in the effect of refraction as light passes into a glass block compared with light moving out of the glass block. Draw diagrams to support your answer.

Learning Outcomes

1.5 Explain how to measure the focal length of a converging lens using a distant object

1.10 Recall that waves are refracted at boundaries between different materials

H 1.11 Explain how waves will be refracted at a boundary in terms of the change of speed and direction

HSW 11 Present information using scientific conventions and symbols

How big did Jupiter look to Galileo?

P1.4 Reflecting telescopes

 How big can we make telescopes?

The largest refracting telescope ever made was built for an exhibition in Paris in 1900. It was 60 m long and had an objective lens that was 1.25 m in diameter. It was dismantled after the exhibition but the lenses can still be seen on display in Paris.

ResultsPlus Watch Out!

It's easy for the words 'reflection' and 'refraction' to look alike. Be careful in your exam when writing thses words.

Reflection in telescopes

Waves are also **reflected** at boundaries between different materials. This means that whenever light passes through a lens, some is reflected. This makes the image fainter. If a star is already very faint, this can be a problem for refracting telescopes.

Refracting telescopes also need to be very long to have large **magnifications**. Large lenses improve the magnification but are very heavy and are difficult to make in a perfect shape, meaning that images have distorted colours. These are not problems in a **reflecting telescope**, which has a curved mirror instead of an objective lens.

A The giant refracting telescope of the 1900 Paris exhibition.

1 State two things that occur when light waves reach a boundary between different materials.

2 Why would a telescope using an objective lens be likely to produce a fainter image of a star than one that uses a mirror?

B When light waves enter a glass block, some light is reflected.

Topic P1.1: Visible light and the Solar System

The curved **primary mirror** focuses parallel light rays from a distant object to an image in the same way as the objective lens in a refracting telescope. This image is then magnified by the eyepiece lens, also just like a refracting telescope. The first reflecting telescope that worked well was produced in 1668 by Sir Isaac Newton (1642–1727).

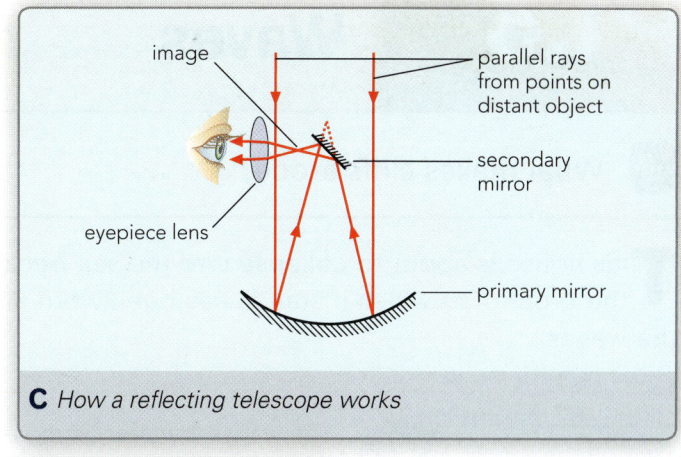

C How a reflecting telescope works

The majority of modern, large telescopes are reflecting. To view very faint, distant stars, a telescope needs to be able to collect tiny amounts of light. This means it needs to have a large diameter primary mirror to allow as much light to enter as possible.

D The primary mirror in the Gemini North telescope has a diameter of 8.1 m and a mass of 22 200 kg.

3 What problems do refracting telescopes suffer with faint stars?

4 Why can reflecting telescopes be shorter than refracting ones that have the same magnification? (*Hint*: Compare Figure C on this page with Figure E on P1.2.)

5 Describe the similarities and differences between the way reflecting and refracting telescopes work.

Skills spotlight

Scientists need to be able to communicate the benefits of their work clearly to the public. You are the director of the Gemini telescope project. A journalist has asked you to justify the huge cost of building the telescope. Write a bullet point list explaining the scientific reasons why a larger diameter mirror is better and why it needs to be a reflecting telescope.

Learning Outcomes

1.10 Recall that waves are reflected at boundaries between different materials

1.8 Explain how the eyepiece of a simple telescope magnifies the image of a distant object produced by the objective lens (ray diagrams are not necessary)

1.9 Describe how a reflecting telescope works

HSW 11 Present information, develop an argument and draw a conclusion, using scientific, technical and mathematical language, and ICT tools

Why shouldn't you build a house near a cliff edge?

P1.5 Waves

  What makes cliffs erode?

This house is about to collapse into the sea because the ground on which it stands has been worn away by the waves.

A *Sea waves carry energy which can wear away a cliff.*

1 If water waves carried matter, what would happen to the water in a swimming pool if you made waves at one end?

Sea waves **transfer** (carry) energy to the shore. When waves hit a cliff, the energy is transferred to the cliff and can wear it away. Waves do not carry matter. Water particles just move up and down as a wave passes – they aren't carried to the shore. Waves in which particles move at right angles to the direction that the wave is going are called **transverse waves**.

B *In a transverse wave the particles move at right angles to the direction the wave is moving.*

C *Sound waves are longitudinal waves.*

D *Wave characteristics*

Electromagnetic waves (such as light, radio waves, microwaves) do not need a medium through which to travel.

Sound waves are not transverse. In a sound wave the particles move back and forth in line with the direction that the wave is going. These are **longitudinal waves**.

Earthquakes and explosions produce **seismic waves** that travel through the Earth. Solid rock material can be pushed and pulled (longitudinal seismic waves) or moved up and down or side to side (transverse seismic waves).

Frequency
Wave **frequency** is the number of waves passing a point each second. It is measured in **hertz** (**Hz**). A frequency of 1 hertz means 1 wave passing per second.

Wavelength
The **wavelength** of a wave is the distance from a point on one wave to the same point on the next wave, measured in metres.

Amplitude
The **amplitude** of a wave is the maximum distance of a point on the wave from its rest position, measured in metres.

44

Wave speed

How fast the energy in a wave travels is the **wave speed**. There are two ways to work this out.

wave speed (metre/second, m/s) = $\dfrac{\text{distance (metre, m)}}{\text{time (second, s)}}$

We can write this as symbols:
$$v = \dfrac{x}{t}$$

> **e.g.** For example, if a wave carries a surfer 52 metres in 8 seconds, the wave speed is:
> $$\text{wave speed} = \dfrac{52}{8} = 6.5\,\text{m/s}$$

The wave speed is also linked to the wave frequency and wavelength:
wave speed (m/s) = frequency (Hz) × wavelength (m)

We can write this as symbols:
$$v = f \times \lambda$$

where λ (the Greek letter lambda) is the symbol for wavelength.

> **e.g.** For example, if some waves of 13-metre wavelength have a frequency of 0.5 Hz then the wave speed is:
> $$v = 0.5 \times 13 = 6.5\,\text{m/s}$$

4 Calculate: **a** the speed of light waves, which travel 900 000 000 m in 3 seconds **b** the speed of sound waves, which have a wavelength of 2 m and a frequency of 170 Hz
H c the wavelength of seismic waves which travel at 5000 m/s and have a frequency of 100 Hz.

H 5 Draw a diagram of a transverse wave to help you explain what is meant by amplitude and wavelength. Then explain what is meant by frequency and wave speed, and how these are connected to the wavelength.

---

2 Give two examples of transverse waves and two examples of longitudinal waves.

3 Sea wave crests pass a stick twice every second. What is the frequency?

Skills spotlight

Scientists need to be able to write instructions for carrying out observations. Write a brief plan for a way to work out the wavelength of waves in the sea if you are at the end of a 50 m pier, and have a stopwatch.

Watch Out!

Take care measuring the amplitude of a wave. It is from the middle to the top or bottom, *not* the distance from crest to trough.

Learning Outcomes

1.12 Describe that waves transfer energy and information without transferring matter

1.13 Use the terms of frequency, wavelength, amplitude and speed to describe waves

1.14 Differentiate between longitudinal and transverse waves by referring to sound, electromagnetic and seismic waves

1.15 Use of both the equations below for all waves:
wave speed (metre/second, m/s) = frequency (hertz, Hz) × wavelength (metre, m)
$v = f \times \lambda$
wave speed (metre/second, m/s) = distance (metre, m)/time (second, s) $v = \dfrac{x}{t}$

HSW 5 Plan to test a scientific idea, answer a scientific question, or solve a scientific problem

Is there any light you can't see?

P1.6 Beyond the visible

 What are infrared and ultraviolet?

For many centuries ships at sea have signalled to each other using lights. The signals are flashes of light that form a code. Remote controls in your home also use this idea but they use flashing signals that you cannot see. They use flashes of infrared waves.

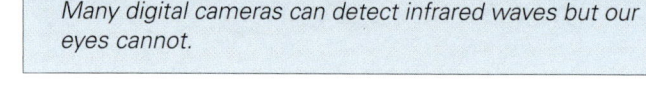

A *An infrared remote control seen on a digital camera screen. Many digital cameras can detect infrared waves but our eyes cannot.*

The discovery of infrared

William Herschel (1738–1822) was a British astronomer. He put dark, coloured filters on his telescope to help him observe the Sun safely. He noticed that different coloured filters heated up his telescope to different extents and he wondered whether the different colours of light contained different 'amounts of heat'.

To test his idea he used a prism to split sunlight into a spectrum, and then put a thermometer in one of the colours. He placed two other thermometers either side of the spectrum. As he changed the colour from violet to red, he found that the temperature rose.

> **Skills spotlight**
>
> It is important for all experiments to have a control. Controls give scientists a way to compare their measurements so that the effects of other variables can be removed from the results. A control uses the same apparatus as the main part of the experiment but the variable that is being changed (the colour of light in this case) is not applied. The two thermometers either side of the spectrum were controls. Suggest a variable that could affect the results of Herschel's experiment.

B *William Herschel and his experiment* (control thermometers)

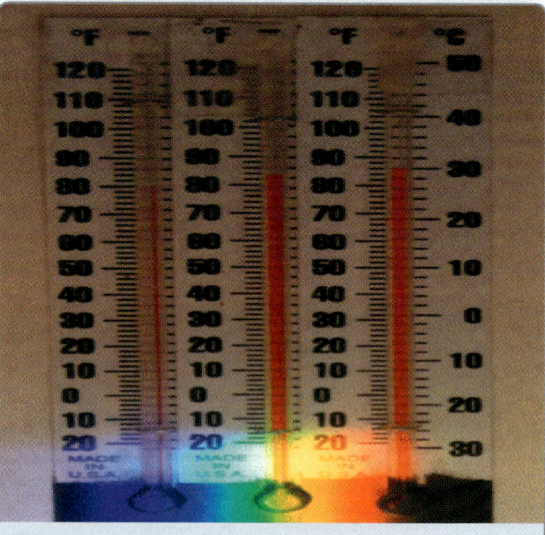

C *It is simple to set up Herschel's experiment today and see the same results.*

Herschel wondered what would happen if he measured the temperature just beyond the red end of the spectrum, where there was no visible light. He found that this gave the highest temperature. He had discovered **infrared** waves (infrared radiation, **IR**).

> 1 List these colours in order of how much they heat up a thermometer: blue, green, orange, red, violet, yellow.
>
> 2 Suggest why Herschel needed to use coloured filters on his telescope.

Going beyond violet

Johann Ritter (1776–1810) found out about Herschel's work and in 1801 set about trying to find 'invisible rays' at the other end of the spectrum. He used silver chloride, a chemical that breaks down to give a black colour when exposed to light.

It was already known that silver chloride turned black more quickly in violet light than in red light. Ritter showed that silver chloride turned black fastest when exposed to 'invisible rays' just beyond violet. These rays were later called **ultraviolet** waves (ultraviolet radiation, **UV**).

> 3 How might Herschel have continued his experiments?
>
> 4 How could Ritter have found out about Herschel's work?

D A bird can see a flower using UV (left) but our eyes only detect visible light (right).

Electromagnetic waves

Visible light, infrared and ultraviolet radiations are all types of **electromagnetic radiation**. The waves transfer energy from one place to another. The electromagnetic vibrations are at right angles to the direction in which the energy is being transferred by the wave (a bit like the water waves in Figure B on P1.5). So they are transverse waves.

> 5 Give two ways in which infrared radiation and ultraviolet radiation are similar types of wave.
>
> 6 Explain how scientists in the middle of the 19th century knew that there is radiation that our eyes cannot detect beyond both ends of the visible spectrum.

Don't get confused by infrared waves, infrared radiation and IR. They are all the same thing!

Learning Outcomes

2.1 Demonstrate an understanding of how Herschel and Ritter contributed to the discovery of waves outside the limits of the visible spectrum

2.2 Demonstrate an understanding that all electromagnetic waves are transverse

HSW 5 Plan to test a scientific idea, answer a scientific question, or solve a scientific problem by controlling relevant variables

P1.7 The electromagnetic spectrum

What is the electromagnetic spectrum?

Sound waves need particles to vibrate in order to transfer energy. Sound cannot travel through space because there are no particles. Electromagnetic waves, like light, can move through space, so we can see the Sun but we cannot hear any sound it makes.

The fastest speed there is

Electromagnetic waves can travel without any particles to vibrate. This means that they can move easily through a **vacuum**, such as space. All electromagnetic waves travel at 300 000 kilometres per second in a vacuum – this is the fastest speed anything can move.

The colour of visible light depends on its wavelength. If the wavelength of a light wave is longer than that of red light, human eyes cannot see it. It is infrared (IR). Microwaves and radio waves have even longer wavelengths than IR.

A A poster from the film Alien. Notice the tagline.

> 1 The Moon is 400 000 km away. How long does it take light reflected from the Moon to reach your eyes?

Electromagnetic waves with shorter wavelengths have higher frequencies. Ultraviolet radiation has a higher frequency than visible light. Even shorter wavelengths are present in **X-rays** and then **gamma rays**.

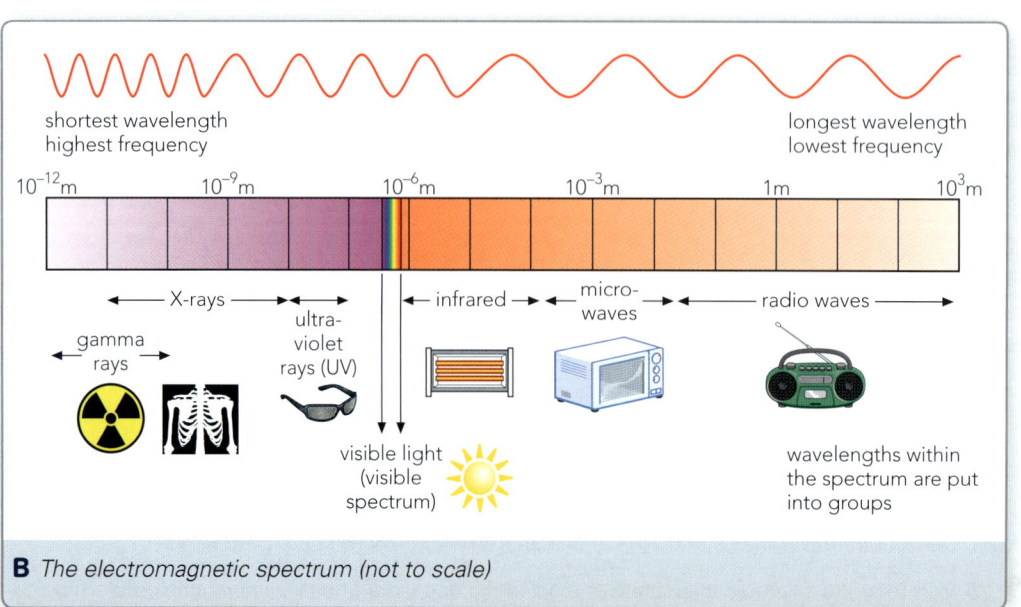

B The electromagnetic spectrum (not to scale)

> 2 Name three different types of electromagnetic waves.
>
> 3 Which part of the electromagnetic spectrum has a higher frequency than X-rays?
>
> 4 What type of electromagnetic wave has a wavelength between visible light and X-rays?

The full range of electromagnetic waves is called the **electromagnetic spectrum**. It's like a bigger version of the visible spectrum and also includes all the wavelengths we cannot see. The spectrum is continuous so all values of wavelength are possible. It is convenient to group the spectrum into seven wavelength groups, as shown in Figure B.

Modern astronomy tries to observe stars and galaxies by detecting the various parts of the electromagnetic spectrum they give off. Radio astronomy and X-ray astronomy are examples that have developed relatively recently. The Hubble Space telescope can detect visible light, UV and IR.

ResultsPlus Watch Out!

Students often get the relationship between frequency and wavelength wrong. Remember that longest wavelength means lowest frequency.

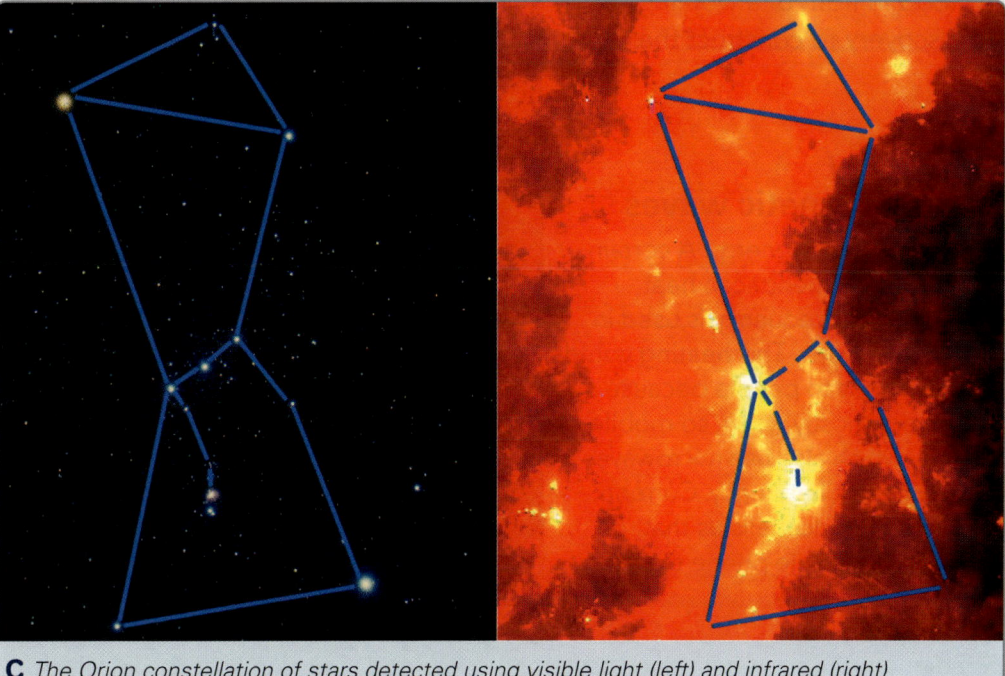

C The Orion constellation of stars detected using visible light (left) and infrared (right)

5 How do we know electromagnetic waves can travel through a vacuum, such as space?

6 List the seven parts of the electromagnetic spectrum in order, and explain how the wavelength, frequency and speed in a vacuum change from one part to the next.

Skills spotlight

Scientists need to be able to analyse their observations to draw conclusions about the Universe. Look at the photographs in Figure C. What conclusions do you think that astronomers drew when they first took IR images of the night sky?

Learning Outcomes

2.2 Demonstrate an understanding that all electromagnetic waves are transverse and that they travel at the same speed in a vacuum

2.4 Demonstrate an understanding that the electromagnetic spectrum is continuous from radio waves to gamma rays, but the radiations within it can be grouped in order of decreasing wavelength and increasing frequency

2.3 Describe the continuous electromagnetic spectrum including (in order) radio waves, microwaves, infrared, visible (including the colours of the visible spectrum), ultraviolet, X-rays and gamma rays

HSW **9** Recall, analyse, interpret, apply and question scientific information or ideas

P1.8 Electromagnetic dangers

 What are the dangers of electromagnetic waves?

In World War II, devices called magnetrons generated microwaves for radar systems to detect German war planes. In 1945, Percy Spencer noticed that a chocolate bar melted in his pocket when he stood in front of a working magnetron. Spencer used this discovery to construct the first microwave oven.

Dangers of electromagnetic waves

All waves transfer energy. A certain microwave frequency can heat water and this frequency is used in microwave ovens. This heating could be dangerous to people because our bodies are mostly water, so mobile phones, which also use microwaves, use a different frequency. Current scientific evidence tells us that, in normal use, mobile phone signals are not a health risk.

A The earliest microwave ovens cost $3000.

IR radiation is used in grills and toasters to cook food. Our skin absorbs IR, which we feel as heat. Too much infrared radiation can damage or destroy cells, causing burns to skin.

> 1 Why should you be careful not to stand too close to a bonfire?
>
> 2 Why do microwave ovens have shields in them to stop the waves escaping?

B Some ways of protecting against the dangers of UV

> 3 Describe two ways to protect yourself against skin damage by UV when in bright sunlight.

Topic P1.2: The electromagnetic spectrum

Higher-frequency waves transfer more energy, and so are potentially more dangerous. Sunlight contains UV, which carries more energy than visible radiation. The energy transferred by UV to our cells can damages their **DNA**. Too much exposure to UV can damage skin cells so much that it leads to **skin cancer**.

The UV in sunlight can also damage our eyes. Skiers and mountaineers can suffer temporary 'snow blindness' because so much UV is reflected from snow.

D This children's warning device changes colour depending upon how much UV it absorbs.

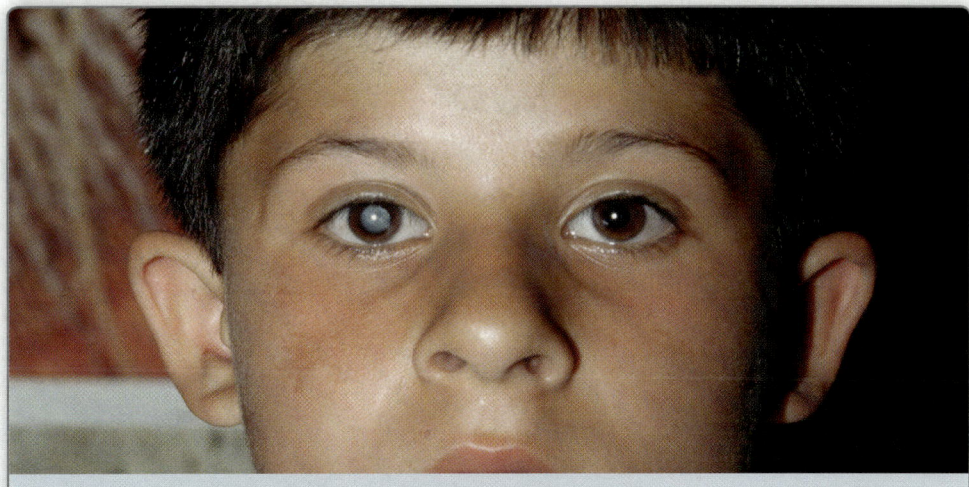

C UV exposure to eyes over a long time can cause cataracts – a clouding of the lens of the eye and reducing vision.

Some parts of the body can absorb X-rays. X-rays are even higher energy than UV. Gamma rays carry even more energy than X-rays. Excessive exposure to X-rays or gamma rays may cause **mutations**, or changes, in DNA which may kill cells or cause cancer.

Skills spotlight

Look at the UV warning device in Figure D. Explain how using the Sun Sensor Watch can help prevent skin cancer.

ResultsPlus Watch Out!

Remember: higher frequency means more energy, which means more danger.

4 Why do people have hospital X-ray photographs taken if X-rays are so dangerous?

5 Why is it useful to have UV predictions in the weather forecast?

6 Draw a table with a row for each part of the electromagnetic spectrum, with increasing frequency down the table. In the second column list any hazards to life that you know for each part of the spectrum. Use your table to explain how the frequency relates to the potential danger.

Learning Outcomes

2.5 Demonstrate an understanding that the potential danger associated with an electromagnetic wave increases with increasing frequency

2.6 Relate the harmful effects, to life, of excessive exposure to the frequency of the electromagnetic radiation, including:
 a microwaves: internal heating of body cells
 b infrared: skin burns
 c ultraviolet: damage to surface cells and eyes, leading to skin cancer and eye conditions
 d X-rays and gamma rays: mutation or damage to cells in the body

HSW 12 Describe the benefits, drawbacks and risks of using new scientific and technological developments

How can highly dangerous gamma rays be useful?

P1.9 Using electromagnetic radiation

 How can the electromagnetic spectrum fight crime?

Many banknotes have a pattern of yellow, green or orange circles. This 'EURion pattern' can be detected by software inside colour photocopiers and scanners, which prevents them from copying the banknotes.

A The coloured pattern on some banknotes prevents digital copying.

Vision and photography

The EURion pattern on banknotes can be seen when **illuminated** because it reflects certain wavelengths of visible light. These wavelengths can be detected by our eyes and by photographic film, digital cameras, photocopiers and scanners.

Security

Other ways of stopping banknotes being counterfeited cannot always be seen. Some materials absorb UV radiation and re-emit it as visible light. This is called **fluorescence**. It is used for security markings on property and banknotes, which can be checked with a UV lamp. **Fluorescent lamps** produce UV waves and use a similar flourescent material on the inside of the bulb glass.

X-ray scanners are used in airports to detect objects hidden on the body as well as in luggage.

All warm objects give off some heat as IR radiation. CCTV cameras that detect IR are used to watch people at night. IR radiation can pass through fog, making **thermal imaging** useful in daytime too.

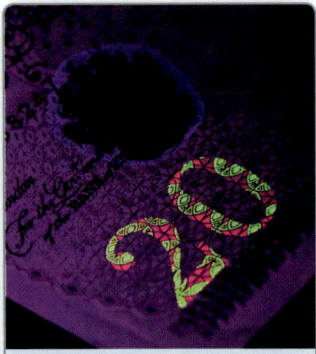

B Forged banknotes can be detected using UV light because they do not have markings that glow. This is a real note.

1 Suggest why fluorescent lamps have fluorescent materials on the inside surface of the bulb glass.

2 Why can't suspects avoid police thermal imaging cameras by hiding in bushes?

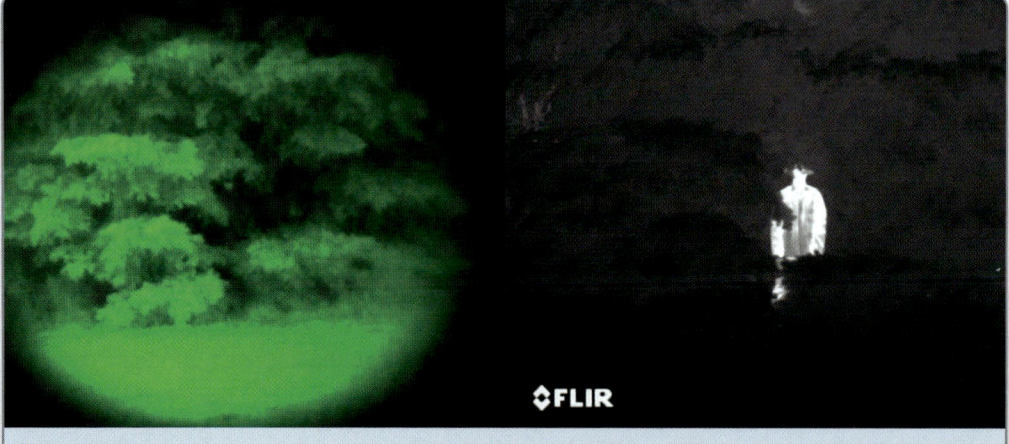

C Both of these photos show the same scene. On the right a suspect is caught by thermal imaging.

Communications

Radio waves are widely used for broadcasting and communications. Microwaves and radio waves carry TV signals, including those from satellites. Wi-Fi™ wireless network connections for computers also use radio waves. Microwaves carry mobile phone signals.

IR waves carry signals a short distance from remote controls to devices like TVs. IR signals are also sent down **optical fibre** cables for telephone and Internet communications.

Food and medicine

Gamma rays transfer a lot of energy, which can kill cells. For this reason, they are used to sterilise food and surgical instruments by killing microorganisms. UV light also kills bacteria, so it can be used to sterilise water and sewage.

Gamma rays are used to kill cancer cells in **radiotherapy**. They can also be used to detect cancer. A chemical that emits gamma rays is injected into the blood. These can be detected by a scanner outside the body. The chemical is designed to collect inside cancer cells and a scanner then locates the cancer by finding the source of the gamma rays.

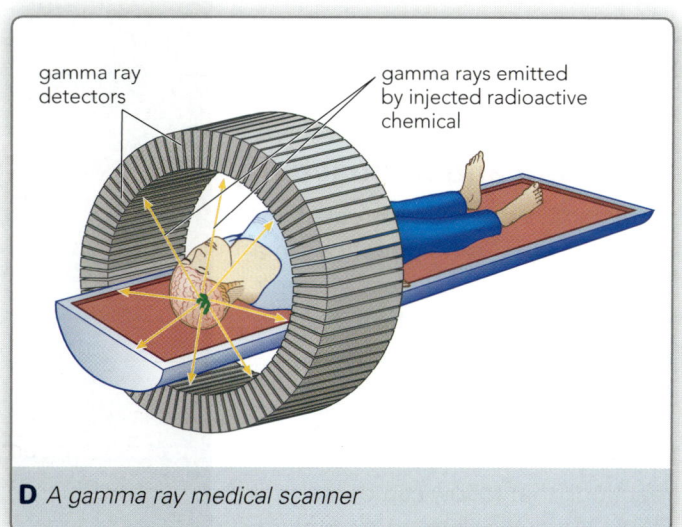

D A gamma ray medical scanner

> **Skills spotlight**
>
> Some people complain that CCTV and whole-body airport scanners are an invasion of their privacy. Discuss the advantages and disadvantages of these kinds of surveillance in society. Try to include any ethical issues about using these technologies.

> **ResultsPlus Watch Out!**
>
> In examinations, students often confuse diagnosis and treatment. The former finds out what is wrong and the latter tries to put it right.

---

3 Why would there be UV lamps at a sewage works?

4 Some people worry when they hear that their herbs have been treated with gamma rays. Why shouldn't they be concerned?

5 Describe two ways gamma rays can be used for medical purposes.

6 Draw a table with a row for each part of the electromagnetic spectrum, with increasing wavelength down the table. In the second column list any uses of each part of the spectrum, with a brief explanation of each application.

Learning Outcomes

2.7 Describe some uses of electromagnetic radiation
  a radio waves: including broadcasting, communications and satellite transmissions
  b microwaves: including cooking, communications and satellite transmissions
  c infrared: including cooking, thermal imaging, short range communications, optical fibres, television remote controls and security systems
  d visible light: including vision, photography and illumination
  e ultraviolet: including security marking, fluorescent lamps, detecting forged bank notes and sterilising water
  f X-rays: including observing the internal structure of objects, airport security scanners and medical X-rays
  g gamma rays: including sterilising food and medical equipment, and the detection of cancer and its treatment

HSW 13 Explain how and why decisions that raise ethical issues about the uses of science and technology are made

>>>>>>> Kryptonite is a fictional green-glowing element from *Superman* stories. Can any real elements glow?

P1.10 Ionising radiation

What is ionising radiation?

In May 1962, the first edition of the science fiction comic book *Incredible Hulk* introduced physicist Dr Bruce Banner. In the book Dr Banner was working for the US Department of Defense to produce a 'gamma bomb'. He was accidentally exposed to a test explosion and became the Hulk. Fifty years later, the US Department of Defense is currently developing just such a bomb. But how would the actual effects of a gamma bomb explosion differ from the fictional ones described in the cartoon?

Radiation and radioactivity

Gamma rays cause an increased risk of cancer by causing mutations in a cell's DNA. This is because gamma rays are **ionising radiation**. Such radiation can remove electrons from atoms to form **ions**. Ions are chemically very reactive. If this happens to atoms in a cell, the reactions that follow can damage the DNA. More exposure to gamma rays can cause the cell to be destroyed. Gamma rays can be used for sterilisation because they destroy bacterial cells.

A *The Incredible Hulk was created by of exposure to gamma ra...*

1 Why are ionising radiations dangerous?

Skills spotlight

A gamma bomb would emit huge amounts of energy in the form of gamma rays. It could kill people directly but would also cause long-term increased risks of cancer for the survivors. Write a paragraph to explain why one country's development of such a bomb might cause other countries to develop similar weapons, and whether you think that this is a good thing or not.

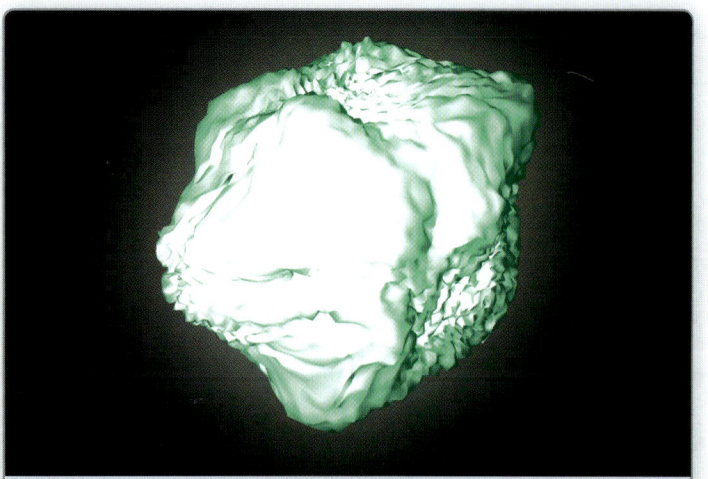

B *Radium metal glows naturally. Radium is radioactive and gives off energy, including gamma rays and visible light, all the time.*

Some elements such as radium naturally emit (give out) gamma (γ) rays all the time. Such elements are said to be **radioactive**. Not all radioactive substances emit gamma waves. Others emit particles, called **alpha (α) particles** and **beta (β) particles**. All three are types of ionising radiation and transfer energy from the radioactive material to their surroundings.

Topic P1.2: The electromagnetic spectrum

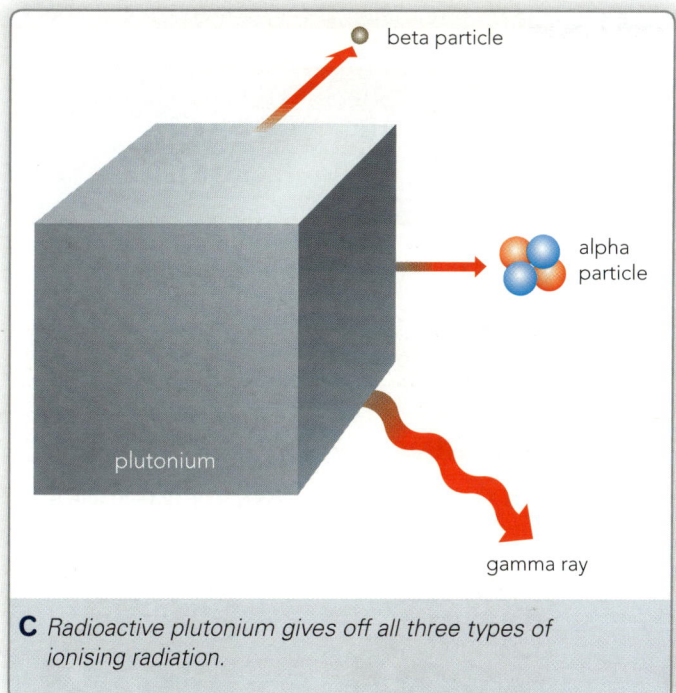

C Radioactive plutonium gives off all three types of ionising radiation.

D Ionising radiation hazard symbol

Alpha particles and beta particles are not electromagnetic radiation. They are particles of matter that are emitted with a lot of kinetic energy. This energy can ionise atoms. So, like gamma rays, alpha and beta particles can be hazardous to life as they can also damage cells and the DNA within the cells.

2 What do the symbols α, β and γ mean?

3 How are alpha, beta and gamma radiations similar?

4 Give two differences between alpha particles and gamma rays.

5 A Geiger–Müller tube is a machine that can detect ionising radiations. Describe how a scientist could test whether a sample of radium emits radiation all the time.

6 Explain why gamma, UV and X-rays can all cause cancer but other parts of the electromagnetic spectrum do not. How do alpha and beta particles fit in with your explanation?

ResultsPlus Watch Out!

Many students say that ionising radiation is only produced by radioactive materials. UV and X-rays can cause cancer because they are also ionising radiations, so they can damage cells and DNA. However, they are not produced by radioactive materials.

Learning Outcomes

2.8 Recall that ionising radiations are emitted all the time by radioactive sources

2.9 Describe that ionising radiation includes alpha and beta particles and gamma rays and that they transfer energy

(HSW) 13 Describe the social, economic and environmental effects of decisions about the uses of science and technology

What's the longest way of writing your address you can think of?

55

More resources for your course

	Science	Additional Science	Extension Units
Student Books	ISBN 978 184690 889 7	ISBN 978 184690 883 5	ISBN 978 184690 886 6
Active Teach with BBC Active Clips Packs (accessible on CD-ROM, via your wVLE or online)	ISBN 978 184690 940 5	ISBN 978 184690 939 9	ISBN 978 184690 938 2
Teacher and Technician Planning Packs	ISBN 978 184690 890 3	ISBN 978 184690 884 2	ISBN 978 184690 887 3
Activity Packs	ISBN 978 184690 888 0	ISBN 978 184690 882 8	ISBN 978 184690 885 9
Teacher Books	ISBN 978 184690 900 9	ISBN 978 184690 901 6	ISBN 978 184690 902 3